The Complete Book of

sushi

The Complete Book of sushi

Hideo Dekura, Brigid Treloar, Ryuichi Yoshii

APPLE

Contents

Recipe list

Introduction

The Japanese believe that food should satisfy all the senses. Food is always prepared with great care and beautifully presented: sometimes very simply, and sometimes in an intricate array. The freshest ingredients are combined in ways that delight the eyes as well as the taste buds. Seasonings are generally quite subtle, in order to enhance the natural flavors.

Sushi combines seasonal seafood and rice, the staple diet of the Japanese people. A wide variety of vegetables can be used in sushi, too. There are more sushi restaurants in Japan than any other type of restaurant, although traditional sushi shops are becoming rare. The increasing number of sushi restaurants outside Japan attests to the worldwide popularity of this delightfully appetizing food.

Because of extensive fishing, refrigerated transport and extremely efficient distribution, no matter where you live in Japan you can eat fresh fish daily, both from Japanese waters and from overseas.

Sashimi means "raw" in Japanese and is generally used to refer to the delicately arranged plates of raw seafood and sliced fresh fish that are served with soy and other dipping sauces. Sushi refers to vinegar-flavored rice topped with sashimi, omelettes and vegetables, or rolled with a variety of fillings in dark green nori seaweed.

Sashimi is usually served as an entree, and sushi as a main course or as the penultimate dish in a Japanese dinner, prior to dessert. Miso soup may be served with sushi. There is an enormous variety of sushi. The ingredients are almost limitless and there are many different ways of making sushi, from traditional forms in which rice and fish are packed together in a container and fermented over a period of time to the most incredible decorative sushi featuring patterns, birds, flowers, fruits and figures. Modern sushi bars most commonly serve maki-zushi, which are bite-sized rolls of sushi rice and seafood or vegetables wrapped in nori seaweed, and nigiri-zushi, which consist of slivers of raw fish or other ingredients laid over bite-sized "bricks" of sushi rice. (Sushi is pronounced "zushi" when it follows a vowel.)

Making sushi is both easy enough to be done at home and so complicated that it takes years for the professional chef to master. If you are a beginner, the recipes for chirashi-zushi and temaki-zushi given in this book may be the easiest to follow initially. Chirashi-zushi is sushi rice and other ingredients served in a bowl; temaki-zushi is hand-rolled cones of nori seaweed (rolled like ice-cream cones) containing sushi rice and various fillings. With some basic equipment, you should have little trouble mastering maki-zushi and, when you are ready for a challenge, you can move on to nigiri-zushi. To make maki-zushi and nigiri-zushi you will need to invest in some of the cooking utensils that are recommended on pages 22–29.

The origins of sushi

The earliest sushi methods probably came to Japan from Southeast Asia or China, at about the time that the Japanese were learning to grow rice. As early as 500 B.C.E., the mountain people in Thailand, Laos and North Borneo used river fish and rice in pickling and fermenting processes that preserved the fish. A similar fermenting process was used in China in early times, but through the reign of Mongolia over China (1368–1644) the process was lost.

In Japan, sushi was seen originally as a way of preserving fish. Layers of carp and layers of rice were placed in a jar with a lid on top and left to ferment for up to a year. The fish would be eaten and the rice thrown away. As time went by, methods of fermentation were developed that took only a few days, so the rice, which had a sharp, sweet taste, could be eaten as well as the fish.

Several centuries ago, the people of Tokyo (or Edo, as it was then called) were known for their businesslike impatience. In the 1640s, they came up with the idea of adding vinegar to the rice to give it a fermented flavor without the bother of having to wait a few days for fermentation to take place. In early sushi making, the fish was either marinated, boiled in soy and mirin, or grilled. In time, the range expanded to include raw fish—sashimi. In the early 1800s, a man called Yohei Hanaya began serving sashimi on sushi rice at his street stall, or yattai, in Tokyo, which marks the beginning of the current style of nigiri-zushi. He brought his fish to his stall in an icebox, which he would then open to show his customers the day's selection.

This yattai stall was a wagon with a counter, and it had a curtain. Until early this century, the most popular sushi stalls were those that had the dirtiest curtains: A dirty curtain meant a busy shop, and therefore a good one. Customers would eat their sushi, dip their fingers in their tea and then wipe their hands on the curtain to dry them. Sushi bar tea cups are large, so they can double as finger bowls. Since the 1950s, sushi has moved indoors to more Western-style, seated establishments. (Even though they no longer serve sushi, you can still visit yattai stalls for cheap outdoor meals in some parts of Japan, particularly in Kyushu.)

As a result of both geography and history, there are many regional differences in Japanese cuisine. Broadly speaking, food prepared in the Kanto region, which includes Tokyo and Yokohama, differs from the Kansai style of Osaka, Kyoto and thereabouts. Kansai-style cooking is seen as "haute cuisine," with subtle flavors, whereas Kanto flavors tend to be stronger, using stronger miso and more soy sauce.

Sushi chefs

Training for sushi chefs is traditionally long and hard. An apprentice spends much of his time with his hands in cold water, doing chores in the kitchen. An apprentice may start training as young as 15 years old and spend the first two years learning to make sushi rice, which in itself requires considerable skill. He will then move on to learning the art of preparing fish, and finally he will actually make sushi.

Until recently, sushi masters were little interested in having students, perhaps because of the potential competition. Often, when the apprentice came to work, the sushi chef would just use him to carry fish home from the market and then as a delivery boy, so the apprentice was never in the bar when sushi were being prepared. A bright apprentice would soon realize what was going on and would have to insist that the sushi chef show him the wide range of skills he needed to acquire.

A trainee learns to be a sushi chef by carefully watching his master at work and then by repeatedly experimenting himself. Eventually, when the apprentice has fully mastered the intricacies of sushi making, he may either work alongside his master or go into business and set up his own sushi bar.

A good sushi chef, in addition to having mastered the standard sushi repertoire, will also be a creative artist. He will be able to create an extensive range of decorative sushi and sashimi in fanciful forms, which may be served on special occasions or for festivals.

Sushi etiquette

Planning a sushi meal

There are a number of different ways sushi can be served, including as an entrée, or as an entire meal consisting of many different varieties. A "roll-your-own" party is another possibility, and sushi is always a welcome treat at picnics.

In planning a sushi meal, consider the following points.

First, sushi is best eaten immediately after rolling. This is also one of the best things about rolling your own sushi cones. As it may not always be possible to make sushi just before guests arrive, prepare all the ingredients required beforehand and make sushi the last item of preparation for the meal. It is best not to leave sushi ingredients at room temperature for more than 2–3 hours before using. Raw fish will require refrigeration.

Second, do not refrigerate sushi rice. Refrigeration changes the quality of the rice—it reduces its starchiness and stickiness, and the rice can become quite hard. To keep sushi rice fresh for a day, cover with a clean muslin cloth (cheesecloth) and keep in a refrigerated container without any ice. Sushi rice should be kept at room temperature for no more than 1 day.

Finally, if raw fish is used, the finished sushi should not be allowed to stand at room temperature for too long. For this reason, it is important to consider the weather, as raw fish may not be appropriate on hot summer days.

A sushi platter may be served for an entrée in a similar manner to an Italian antipasto platter. The platter can include hand rolls, hand-shaped sushi (nigiri-zushi), and possibly inside-out sushi with gari (pickled ginger), wasabi, and leaf decorations. It is best to prepare the platter no more than 1 hour before consuming. As sushi is decorative in appearance, arrange rolls attractively to showcase their artistic qualities. Individual plates of sushi, with about 4 pieces per serving, can also make an attractive and fast entrée.

Hand-roll party

Do-it-yourself hand rolls allow the party organizer to simply prepare the ingredients and enjoy the rest of the party. If making sushi for a children's party, you may choose special ingredients, excluding wasabi, for example. If using raw fish, remove it from the refrigerator at the last minute, place it on a bed of ice, and cover it with a bamboo sushi mat.

Picnic

If a picnic is planned, a lunch box including sushi is a pleasant alternative to sandwiches. Because of possible spoilage, it is better not to use raw fish for picnics. Suggested ingredients are omelettes, cooked shrimp (prawns), avocado, smoked salmon, fresh vegetables such as cucumber and carrots, pickles, and cheese. They should be kept in a refrigerated container until ready to consume. Small plastic bottles are good for soy sauce and other essential dipping sauces. Alternatively, prepare the ingredients and wrap them separately in plastic wrap, then have family or friends roll their own sushi cones.

Main meal

Sushi can be prepared as a main meal in a similar fashion as an entrée by serving more substantial amounts of a variety of sushi, attractively displayed, on a large platter. Don't forget to provide individual dishes for dipping sauces.

Desserts

Gelatin desserts, pieces of fresh fruit, or sorbet are perfect treats after a sushi meal. They are light and refreshing, and provide a good balance to the sushi.

Serving sushi

All meals are made to be savored. One of the pleasures of eating foods from other cultures is the different customs they have at the tables. Here you are provided with the traditional ways of eating sushi; some you'll adopt, others you won't. Either way, sushi is a meal to share and enjoy.

Sushi is made with the fingers and can be eaten with the fingers or with chopsticks. It is presented in artful arrangements on a platter or as individual dishes and served with gari (pickled ginger slices) and wasabi (Japanese horseradish) on the side. Gari is eaten between different types of sushi to cleanse the palate. Fiery wasabi is used in many varieties of sushi and also added to sushi by diners according to taste. Be sure to provide individual bowls of Japanese soy sauce (shoyu) for dipping. Although there are six varieties of Japanese soy sauce, only two are commonly used. Both heavy soy sauce (koikuchi shoyu) and light soy sauce (usukuchi shoyu) are used in cooking. Heavy soy sauce is the variety supplied separately at the table. Chinese soy sauce should not be substituted for the Japanese variety, as the flavor can be too strong and often too salty. Contrary to popular belief, wasabi should not be mixed into the soy sauce when eating sushi, as it dilutes the two flavors. Place a small amount of wasabi on the sushi with a finger or chopstick, then dip into the sauce.

Sushi can be served alone as an appetizer or light meal or as a course in a larger meal. A simple yet complete sushi meal combines sushi with miso or suimono (clear) soup and pickles, and fresh fruit for dessert—and, of course, green tea. Suimono, which means "something to drink," can be served as a first course or part-way through a meal as a palate refresher. Simple, natural and fresh, it should not dull the appetite but stimulate the taste buds to appreciate all the delicate flavors. It should be impressive in its purity and restraint. The heartier miso soup can be a meal in itself, and should be served with or after the sushi. If possible, serve Japanese soups, both thick and thin, in covered lacquer bowls, which keep the soup hot but allow the bowl to stay cool enough to be picked up.

Japanese desserts are very simple, if served at all. Fresh fruit, decoratively cut and beautifully presented, provides an elegant finish to a sushi meal. Today, green tea ice cream is often served to cleanse and refresh the palate.

Hot green tea is considered essential to the full enjoyment of sushi as it also cleanses the palate and refreshes the mouth, removing any aftertaste between bites. The thick tea cups used for Japanese tea are leftover from the days of outdoor stalls, where water was often in short supply and busy proprietors found it more efficient to pour green tea into a large, heat-retaining cup so it had to be topped up less often.

Traditionally, an unlimited supply of green tea is served throughout the meal. Beer, sake and more recently, white wine, have become popular also. Sake, like wine, can be either sweet or dry, and may be drunk chilled or warm. The choice is a matter of personal taste, and although sake has always been considered a must in Japan, there are divided opinions about serving it with sushi, as both are made from rice.

Traditional customs

• Green tea is normally served at the beginning of and then throughout a meal.

• It is acceptable practice to slurp hot tea and soup as a sign of enjoyment and to blow on the liquid to cool it.

• When giving or receiving food it is polite to use both hands when lifting the bowl or plate.

• Place chopsticks in front of guests, side by side, with both points on a chopstick rest facing to the left. Chopsticks that face to the right are a symbol of bad luck.

• The tips of chopsticks should never touch the table. Always use chopstick rests, which can be as simple as a folded napkin or the paper sleeve from the chopsticks.

• If using new, disposable wooden or bamboo chopsticks, have diners split apart and scrape one against the other to remove any splinters before use.

• Where possible, garnishes and table decorations should reflect the season.

• If no serving utensils are provided, diners should use the handle end of individual chopsticks to take food from a communal dish. They then set the sushi onto their individual plate.

• Japanese plates rarely match in the manner of a Western dinner service. Plates are chosen for color, shape and texture to complement the food served.

• Never fill serving platters, individual plates or dipping bowls to capacity, as this is considered rude. Be prepared to refill dipping bowls as needed.

• A Japanese meal is normally served all at once rather than in courses. Small portions are taken from platters at random. While anything not liked can be left, it is considered bad manners to leave any rice on the plate, because rice is held in such high regard and has been the main food of Japan for centuries.

• It is quite acceptable to eat sushi with fingers. In Japan sushi is sometimes served without chopsticks, as it is assumed that fingers only will be used.

• Lift nigiri-zushi (see page 94) upside down if eaten with fingers or on its side if eaten with chopsticks. Dip the topping in sauce so it comes into contact with taste buds first, followed by the seasoned rice.

• You should never pour your own drinks. Offer to serve others and wait for someone to offer to fill your cup or, if someone fills your cup, do likewise for them.

• An empty glass or cup means you would like a refill. If you don't want any more leave it full.

• Sake is to the Japanese as wine is to the French. There are different sakes of different grades. Drink sweet or dry heated to 105–120°F (40–50°C) or chilled.

• Always lift the sake cup when it is being filled from the sake bottle.

• Moisten and wring out a small hand towel, heat in the microwave or in a bamboo steamer and offer at the beginning and end of a Japanese meal for guests to refresh themselves.

Eating sushi at a sushi bar

At a sushi bar, you can order your food from a menu or choose items from the refrigerated glass case in front of you. Often, it is best to rely on the sushi chef's advice. The selection of fish at the markets varies from day to day, and as he will have selected the fish himself, the sushi chef will be able to recommend the freshest and best sushi to you, and serve them in the most appropriate order. You may wish to start your meal with sashimi and have a bowl of miso soup with your sushi.

On the plate with the sushi, you will be given a small heap of wasabi, a spicy condiment, and a small heap of slices of pickled ginger (gari). Served alongside will be a small bowl of soy sauce. With your meal, it is traditional to drink tea. Japanese tea is generally called ocha. When drunk with sushi it is called agari.

Sushi is often served with decorations made from bamboo or aspidistra leaves (a smooth, stemless Asian herb bearing large evergreen leaves) and at some sushi bars leaves are used instead of plates. The leaf decorations serve a practical purpose in separating sushi pieces and are a means of demonstrating the chef's cutting skills.

When eating nigiri-zushi, it is traditional to use your hands and then wipe them on a towel. You may also use chopsticks. Take a dab of wasabi on your chopstick, gently pick up a piece of sushi and dip the end of the topping in the bowl of soy sauce. Do not dip the rice side of the sushi in the soy as you will simply taste soy, rather than the flavors of both rice and topping. Put the sushi in your mouth with the topping side down—so the fish meets your taste buds. (Do not mix the wasabi in the soy sauce, as you will drown the sushi with the flavor of the wasabi.)

Maki-zushi can be eaten either with your hand or with chopsticks, picking the roll up at the sides.

After eating a piece of sushi, eat a slice of pickled ginger to clean your palate, have a sip of tea, then eat the next piece of sushi. Japanese green tea removes oiliness after eating fish and prepares the palate for the next piece. Sushi bars serve tea that has a slightly bitter flavor—sweet tea should be avoided, as it diminishes the flavor of the sushi.

Nowadays, people drink beer, wine or sake with sushi. Sake, the traditional Japanese drink made from fermented rice, comes in a variety of styles. It varies from dry to sweet, like wine, and may be drunk chilled or hot. For sushi, try subtle styles of sake which will not overpower the fresh tastes. Delicately flavored white wines will also balance well with sushi, enhancing and complementing the flavors.

When you receive your bill, do not be too shocked at the total. The best sushi bars sell only the highest quality fresh fish, which is becoming increasingly expensive.

Health benefits of sushi

Sushi, an exquisite food, is also one of the healthiest and most nutritional foods available. Fish, rice, vegetables, soy and nori are basic sushi ingredients, all readily available and all excellent nutritionally.

Fish and seafood are highly nutritious and low in calories (kilojoules). Just a small portion of fish supplies between one-third and half of the protein we require daily. Most fish and seafood are excellent sources of vitamin B12, which is essential for building and maintaining cells, and of iodine, which is needed for the thyroid gland to work effectively. Seafood such as shrimp (prawns) and squid are high in cholesterol, so are best eaten only in small quantities by people who need to limit their cholesterol intake. It appears, however, that crab and oysters lower blood cholesterol.

Oily fish, such as tuna and salmon, are a rich source of omega-3 fatty acids, which are highly beneficial in the prevention of heart disease and stroke.

Rice is the main food for more than half the world's population. It is a good source of protein and carbohydrate and, because it is digested slowly, it releases energy gradually. It has the additional benefit of being gluten-free, so it can be eaten by people who are wheat-intolerant.

Vinegar has antibacterial qualities and has long been used to preserve food. It also has an extensive history in certain cultures as a tonic. It is used as an aid to digestion, prevents fatigue and lessens the risk of high blood pressure.

Nori seaweed is rich in vitamins and minerals, notably iodine, and helps to curb the formation of cholesterol deposits in the blood vessels.

Ginger and wasabi, like vinegar, have antibacterial properties. Ginger aids digestion and helps reinforce the body's defenses against colds and flu. Wasabi is rich in vitamin C.

Soybeans, which are used to make tofu and fermented products such as soy sauce, miso and natto, are high in protein, magnesium, potassium and iron. Soy products also contain phytoestrogens that act in a similar way to estrogen, one of the female hormones. Soybeans have been used successfully in the treatment of premenstrual and menopause problems. Soy sauce is high in salt and can also contain wheat, so should be avoided by people who have problems digesting gluten.

Vegetables are an excellent source of vitamins, minerals and fibre. In addition, it has been shown that there is a lower incidence of cancer in populations where a good quantity of fruit and vegetables are consumed. Plants contain compounds known as phytochemicals, which help protect the body from disease.

There is another very important factor that adds to the nutritional benefits of eating sushi. It is a well-known dieting procedure that chewing your food well aids in digestion and makes you feel less hungry. Sushi rice is fairly firm and therefore requires chewing longer. This allows the appetite nerve center of the brain to receive the signals of satiety, and hence aids in eating less!

Remember, one of the healthy ways of eating food is in a pleasant atmosphere. Whether in a sushi bar, with the chatter of the sushi chef and customers, or at home, the practice of sharing balanced and beautiful food makes for a wonderful and healthy experience.

Equipment and utensils

The following items are recommended for making sushi and are obtainable from Japanese specialty stores and some larger Asian supermarkets. In many cases, you will find that substitutes from your kitchen cupboards are suitable. For making sushi rolls, a bamboo rolling mat is essential, and if you have tweezers, a fish scaler and high-quality knives you will find handling and filleting fish a great deal easier.

Bamboo rolling mat (makisu)

The simple rolling mat used for making sushi rolls is made of thin strips of bamboo woven with cotton string. After you have used the mat, scrub it down with a brush and dry it thoroughly, otherwise it may become moldy. For easier cleaning, wrap the mat in plastic wrap and discard the plastic after use. It is best to buy an all-purpose mat measuring 12 x 12 inches (30 x 30 cm), but smaller ones are also available. When making sushi, the mat must be dry.

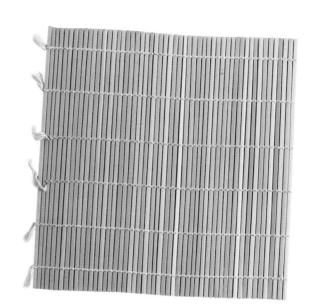

Bowl with lid

A large bowl with a lid is needed for holding the cooked sushi rice once it has been prepared, to keep it warm. An insulated bowl is ideal.

Chopping board

A chopping board is needed for a variety of tasks, from preparing fish and vegetables to assembling all the different sorts of sushi. Traditionally, a wooden chopping board was used, but resin boards are widely available and are easier to keep free of odors.

It is best to have a board measuring at least 10 inches x 15 inches (25 cm x 38 cm).

Chopsticks (saibashi)

The chopsticks used for cooking are two to three times longer than chopsticks used for eating. Cooking chopsticks are extremely useful implements, once you have mastered the technique, as they enable you to manipulate food using only one hand.

Fan (uchiwa)

An uchiwa is a flat fan made of paper or silk stretched over light bamboo ribs, and is traditionally used for cooling and separating the sushi rice. While it is delightful to own an uchiwa, a piece of heavy paper or cardboard will do the job just as well.

Fish scaler

When cleaning and preparing fish at home, it is easiest to use a scaler, available from a fish market. Simply draw it up the body of the fish, working from tail to head. Do not use the back of a cleaver as a substitute, as you run the risk of bruising the fish.

Grater

Sushi chefs use a length of sharkskin for grating wasabi root; for grating pieces of ginger and daikon, they use a ceramic bowl that has small teeth on the surface.

If you are using a straightforward household grater, a flat one made of stainless steel is most suitable. Be sure to choose one that is comfortable to hold and has closely packed, sharp teeth. When using the grater, particularly when grating ginger, use a circular motion.

Knives

Japanese chefs use knives that are traditionally made from the same steel that was used to make samurai swords. They are renowned for their strength and sharpness (see page 28 for sharpening Japanese knives).

The best sort of knife to use for filleting fish and for slicing pieces of fish for sashimi and sushi is a long, slender one with a pointed end. A wide, heavy knife is useful for cutting through bone, as when removing a fish's head. Never use a serrated knife when cutting fish, as it will tear the flesh, spoiling its appearance. For chopping and slicing vegetables, a long, square-ended cleaver is most suitable.

Sharp, strong, good-quality steel knives are needed for the best results.

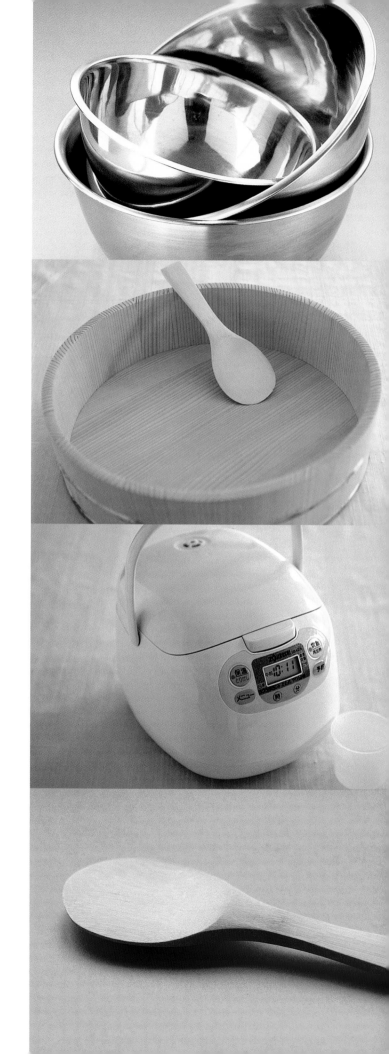

Mixing bowls

You will need several mixing bowls. Stainless steel ones are recommended.

Mortar and pestle (suribachi and surikogi)

Japanese mortars have a textured grooved pattern on an unglazed interior. This works like the surface of a grater when struck with a pestle. Japanese mortars are easier to use than conventional, smooth-surfaced mortars. Use the tip of a bamboo skewer to clean the grooves.

Plates for sushi

When serving sushi, you need a set of plates that are as flat as possible. If the rim of a serving plate is curved or ridged, the presentation of the sushi will not be as attractive and they will probably fall over.

Rice-cooling tub (hangiri)

The broad, wooden hangiri, generally made of cypress, and with low sides, is designed specifically for cooling sushi rice. This gives the rice the ideal texture and gloss, but a non-metallic flat-bottomed bowl can be used instead. The bigger the bowl the better, as you will then be able to stir and separate the rice grains properly.

If you are using a hangiri, wash it well after use, dry it carefully, then wrap it in a cloth and store it face downward in a cool, dry place.

Rice maker

An electric or gas rice maker is highly recommended for cooking rice, as it will control the temperature and cooking time to give perfect rice every time. Otherwise, use a heavy pot with a tight-fitting lid.

Rice paddle (shamoji)

This flat paddle is made of wood or plastic, and is often supplied with rice cooker. Because it is flat, it can slice through rice when mixing it without squashing the grains.

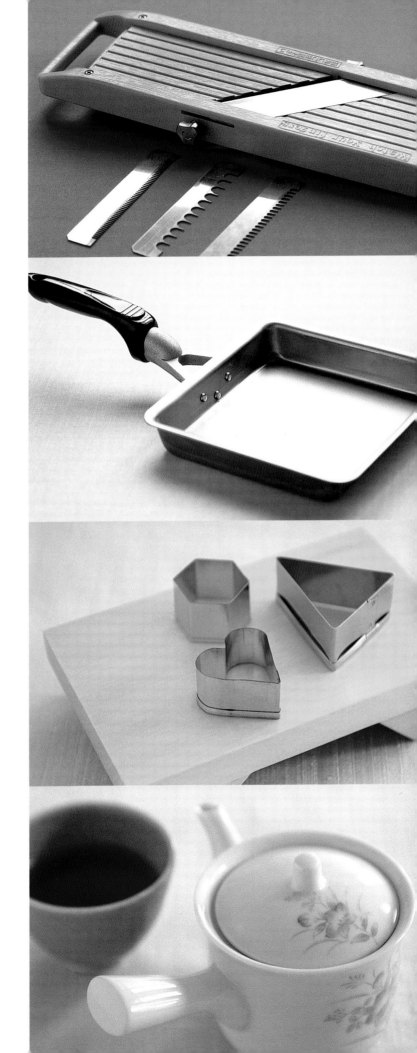

Shredder/slicer

A Japanese shredder has a selection of three blades to vary width and an adjustable dial to alter the depth of shredding. Use the wide blade to julienne vegetables and the narrow blade to shred daikon and carrot for garnishes. Remove blades to use as a slicer. Larger and circular shredders are also available for creating long continuous shreds.

Skewers

When cooking shrimp, it is best to use either bamboo skewers or long toothpicks.

Stainless-steel colander

A colander is used for straining rice and for washing and draining other ingredients.

Square omelette pan

A square-shaped omelette pan about 1 inch (3 cm) deep is traditionally used for making sushi omelettes. A thick pan that retains heat is ideal, but can be heavy to handle. You can use a conventional round skillet about 10 inches (25 cm) in diameter and trim the sides of the omelette once it has been cooked, to make it square.

Sushi molds

Usually wood or plastic for home use, and available in different shapes and sizes. Dip molds in water with a splash of rice vinegar to stop sushi rice sticking to mold.

Teacup and teapot (kyusu to yunomi)

Japanese teacups and teapots can be found in most kitchenware shops. The most pleasing teapot and teacups are fine porcelain. Japanese teapots have a very fine-mesh strainer, which is either built into the base of the spout or is part of a removable basket. They are small compared with Western teapots. In sushi bars, Japanese tea is served in a deep, narrow pottery cup with no handle; the cup may be inscribed with the logo of the sushi bar.

Tempura pan (tempura nabe)

A tempura pan has fairly straight sides, and is approximately 4 inches (10 cm) deep. It has a removable wire-mesh draining rack attached to the pan, which keeps the cooked tempura warm and allows the oil to drain. A wok can also be used (some woks also have draining racks).

Tweezers

Heavy, straight-ended tweezers come in handy for deboning fish. These are obtainable from a fish market. Alternatively, use tweezers purchased from a drugstore.

Vegetable cutters (kata)

Flower-shaped cutters are available from Japanese stores. Cookie cutters can be substituted.

Vegetable peeler (kawamuki)

The Japanese peeler is similar to a potato peeler, but the blade is set at a right angle to the handle, which makes it easy to slice vegetables in thin, long strips that are suitable for wrapping sushi (see picture, at left).

Sharpening Japanese knives

Houchou, the Japanese knife, is sharper and cuts faster and sharper than Western knives. The single-edged blade, its main characteristic, is usually on the right side, for right-handed use. Left-edged blades can be ordered.

There are three grades of blades in Japan: honyaki, hongasumi, and kasumi. Grading is based upon the length of time the knife remains sharp. Honyaki is the highest quality, as the pure carbon steel blades retain their original sharpness for the longest period. Hongasumi and kasumi blades are both made with a combination of soft iron and carbon steel. Their softer iron outer layer facilitates sharpening.

When sharpening a Japanese knife, have a whetstone that is used with water rather than with oil. Soak Japanese whetstones in water for about 20 minutes before sharpening blades.

Sashimi knife
The yanagiba-bouchou has a carbon steel blade about 16 inches (40 cm) long. Commonly called a "sashimi knife," it is used for filleting small and medium-sized fish. A stainless steel filleting knife, about 8 inches (20 cm) long, or a chef's knife, can be substituted.

Vegetable carving knife
This knife, the usuba-bouchou, is designed specifically for slicing and cutting vegetables. The blade touches the vegetable surface at a right angle, and the vegetable clings to the blade. A Western filleting knife with a stainless steel blade about 6½ inches (16.5 cm) can be substituted.

Filleting knife
The deba-bouchou, used for filleting fish, is much heavier than other knives. This weight permits a particularly sharp cut. The 16-inch (40-cm) length includes both blade and grip. This is the first knife you should purchase for preparing sashimi. Or substitute a Western filleting or paring knife with a stainless steel blade about 5 inches (13 cm) long.

Top to bottom: Sashimi knife, vegetable carving knife, filleting knife

1 Place whetstone on wet towel to hold it in place. Wipe clean with damp towel and hold knife in right hand. Place top half of blade flat on stone at a 40-degree angle to the body. Placing middle and index fingers on blade, apply pressure, and move blade forward and backward. Wipe blade.

2 Once the top is sharpened, proceed to score the base of the blade.

3 As most Japanese knives are single-edged, when blades are honed the shaved pieces cling to the flat side of the blade. To remove, turn the knife, place edge of blade on corner of stone at a 45-degree angle. Slide blade down to remove excess metal.

4 Wipe knife clean with a damp towel.

Note: Steps are written for right-edged blade. Check sharpness regularly.

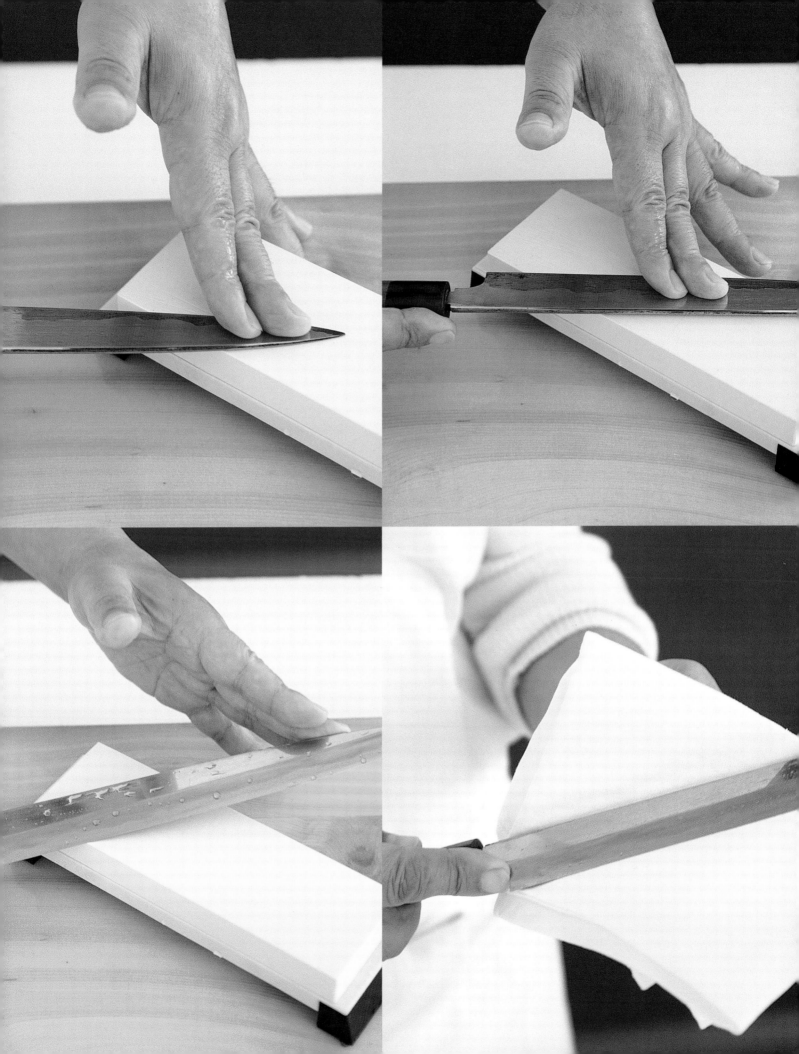

Ingredients

Avocado

Bonito flakes (katsuo boshi)

Daikon radish

Japanese people, on the whole, love to live in harmony with nature and therefore favor eating fresh foods in season. In keeping with this attitude, and for the best results, use the freshest foods possible when making sushi.

The range of possible ingredients for sushi is vast, limited only by what is available and the cook's imagination. There are, of course, many traditional ingredients, some of which may be new to you, but they will generally be obtainable from Asian food stores and larger supermarkets.

Traditionally, sushi has been largely fish-based, but ingredients other than fish and seafood are becoming increasingly popular. Tofu is a recent arrival in the repertoire, as are snow pea sprouts and other types of sprout. When selecting vegetables for sushi, go to the best-quality store in your neighborhood and choose only the freshest, firmest produce, as generally it is served either raw or blanched.

Japanese ingredients are highly recommended—soy sauce, sake, sushi vinegar and other seasonings—as they are made traditionally to suit Japanese foods. Substituting other ingredients will result in different flavors.

Aji-ponzu

A yellow-colored vinegar that tastes particularly good with salmon. Ponzu is the name of a lemon and soy dipping sauce that can be bought ready-made.

Aka oroshi

Japanese red chili paste. This is mixed with grated daikon radish and used as a garnish for white-fish sushi. Do not substitute other types of chili paste, as they will probably be too pungent.

Asparagus

Choose asparagus with straight stalks and good color. Blanch in salted, boiling water and cut into 2–4 inch (5–10 cm) lengths before using; cut them lengthwise into several slices if they are thick.

Avocado

Use avocados that are ripe but firm. The best ones for sushi have a thin, smooth skin and green and gold flesh. Before being used for sushi, avocados are thinly sliced.

Bonito flakes (katsuo boshi)

These sandy brown flakes of smoked, dried and fermented bonito fish are used to make dashi, which is a basic Japanese stock.

Carrots

Select carrots that are crisp and bright orange. Peel them and cut into lengths of 2–4 inches (5–10 cm) before slicing. Carrots can be made into the most intricate decorations.

straight leaves. Peel them deep enough to remove both the skin and the fibers beneath it. Daikon contains various enzymes and is good for the digestion when eating strongly flavored oily foods. Cut into fine slivers, it is eaten with sashimi; paper-thin slices are rolled around sashimi in place of nori seaweed; and grated daikon is added to soy sauce and other sauces for texture and flavor. It is also grated and piled on the serving plate. Daikon radish sprouts are called kaiware, and are delicious in salads and sandwiches.

Eggplant (aubergine) Enoki mushrooms Seasoned carrots

Chili seasonings

See aka oroshi. Ichimi togarashi is mild Japanese chili powder. Do not use other forms of chili paste or powder as substitutes, as they will probably be too strong.

Chives

This herb is used in 1-inch (2.5-cm) slices in sashimi rolls and is minced to garnish white-fish sushi.

Cucumber

Japanese cucumbers are about 6–8 inches (15–20 cm) long. They are less watery than American cucumbers and have fewer seeds, firmer insides and softer skins. If you can't find Japanese cucumbers, use a 6–8 inch (15–20 cm) piece of European (hothouse) cucumber. Buy firm-skinned cucumbers with a medium green color.

Daikon radish

A Japanese giant white radish with a smooth skin, at least 20 inches (50 cm) long. Daikon is less pungent than many radishes. Look for firm, shiny ones with smooth skin and

Eel

Fresh eel is not widely available: much of it worldwide is exported to Japan, where it is made into unagi—eel prepared in the Japanese manner. Unagi is steamed and then broiled, after being brushed with soy sauce and mirin. You can buy frozen unagi eel at Asian supermarkets.

Eggplant (aubergine)

Japanese eggplants are similar to Chinese eggplants, which are smaller and thinner than Italian (globe) eggplants. They are usually 6–8 inches (15–20 cm) long and about 2 inches (5 cm) in diameter. Choose firm, purple, smooth-fleshed ones with straight stalks. If using a larger eggplant, peel off the skin. Eggplant should be sliced, then lightly grilled or fried before being used in sushi.

Enoki mushrooms

These white mushrooms have long, thin stalks and tiny caps. Choose ones that are crisp and white. Yellowish brown ones are old and should be avoided. Cut off the "roots" at the bottom of the stalks.

Gari

Ginger slices that have been pickled in salt and sweet vinegar. They are a delicate pink color and are available in bottles and other forms of packaging. The bright red vinegared ginger is not used with sushi. Small amounts of gari are eaten between bites of sushi to freshen the palate.

Ginger

The thick, rootlike rhizome of the ginger plant has a sharp, pungent flavor. Ginger should be firm, with a smooth skin.

Kombu

Dried kelp. This sea vegetable is available in the form of hard, flat, black sheets that have a fine white powder on the surface. Kombu is used to flavor dashi, a basic soup stock, and sushi rice. Wipe the surface of the sheets with a damp cloth before use to remove the powder. Do not wash the kombu; this will diminish its flavor. Avoid kombu that is wrinkled and thin.

Kampyo   Kombu   Seasoned lotus root

Once the thin, tan skin is peeled away from fresh ginger, the flesh is sliced or grated. Store fresh ginger in the refrigerator. Grated ginger is used to garnish white-fish sushi. See also gari.

Kaiware

See daikon radish.

Kamaboko

Japanese-style fish cakes, available frozen. There are various forms, some of them dyed pink. Kamaboko can be used in chirashi-zushi.

Kampyo

Dried bottle gourd or calabash, used in the form of shavings or ribbonlike strips. Before being used in sushi, kampyo is tenderized and seasoned.

Kimchi

Korean spicy fermented cabbage. Kimchi is strongly flavored, so use only a small quantity.

Lotus root (renkon)

The crunchy root of the lotus plant is used in a variety of Japanese dishes, including chirashi-zushi. It is peeled, then sliced before cooking. The slices resemble white wheels with holes in them. It discolors as soon as it is cut, so place slices in water to which 1 teaspoon vinegar has been added. Fresh lotus root can be found at most Asian markets. Vinegared lotus root is available in packets.

Mayonnaise

Mayonnaise goes well with certain sushi, but be sure to use either homemade egg mayonnaise or commercially available mild-flavored creamy egg mayonnaise. It can be mixed with soy sauce as a garnish for California rolls.

Mirin

Sweet alcoholic wine made from rice. Store in a cool, dark place after opening. If mirin is unavailable, use 1 teaspoon sugar in place of 1 tablespoon mirin.

Miso

A fermented mixture of soybeans, salt and water and a fermenting agent—usually soy "koji," rice or barley. There are many types and mixtures of miso, but they can be broadly divided into three categories: sweet, nonsweet and salty. White miso, the sweetest, is ivory to yellow in color and is seldom available outside Japan. What is commonly known as white miso is golden colored and has a mild flavor. Red miso is aged the longest and is the salty form. White and red miso, plus many blends, are available in Asian supermarkets.

Ocha

Japanese tea. The kind served with Japanese meals is generally green tea. Bancha and sencha are types of green tea, and are available in leaf and powdered form or in teabags. Bancha should steep for 2–3 minutes; sencha should steep for 1 minute only. Gyokuro and other expensive green teas are not suitable for serving with sushi. When served with sushi, ocha is known as agari.

Mirin   Miso   Natto

Mustard cress

Mustard cress is a mixture of the sprouts of white mustard seeds and cress. Cress is produced from the seeds of a plant native to Europe and is related to the pepperwort. It has small bright green leaves on tender white stalks. Cress tastes hot and peppery. Mustard cress is available in supermarkets.

Natto

Fermented soybeans. Natto has a rich flavor, similar to cheese, a pungent odor and a rather glutinous consistency. In Japan, it is used as a flavoring and table condiment and many Japanese enjoy natto served over rice for breakfast.

Nori

Sheets of seaweed used for making rolls. The sheets measure about 7½ x 8 inches (19 x 20.5 cm) and are sold in cellophane or plastic bags. Once the wrapping has been opened, use the nori as soon as possible or store it in a container in a cool place. Make sure you buy precooked nori, known as yaki-nori, which is dark green. The black or purple types of nori are raw and must be toasted over a flame.

Okra

This vegetable, sometimes known as gumbo, comes in the form of five-sided pods that taper to a point, with a flowerlike cross-section filled with seeds. Choose crisp, young okra, 2–4 inches (5–10 cm) long. It keeps for 2 or 3 days in the refrigerator, loosely wrapped in plastic. Okra is boiled, then cut in half lengthwise for use in sushi.

Quail eggs

Considered a delicacy in Asia, quail eggs can be found in specialty markets and in some supermarkets. Their dainty size means they are popular on hors d'oeuvres, usually hard-boiled.

Rice

Short-grain white rice. Use Japanese rice or California short-grain rice. The size, consistency, taste, and smell of other types of rice are not suitable for making sushi.

Sake

Japanese fermented rice wine. Sake is used in cooking to tenderize meat and fish, and to make ingredients more flavorful. It also counteracts acidity. Buy cooking sake (ryori sake) or inexpensive drinking sake for making sushi.

Salt

Rock salt or sea salt is best.

Scallions (shallots/spring onions)

Buy thin, straight, moist shoots that are firm and crisp. The Japanese use most of the green part of scallions, discarding only the very tip. Chopped scallions are used as a garnish.

looks decorative. If using dried shiitake mushrooms, choose brown-capped ones that have been well dried and are therefore cracked-looking. Soak them in water for at least 30 minutes before using. The longer they are soaked, the softer they become. When soaked, good-quality shiitake mushrooms are fleshy and plump.

Shiso

This aromatic herb, a member of the mint family, is known in the West as perilla. Buy fresh, green leaves. There is also a red variety that is used for coloring and flavoring umeboshi and other Japanese pickles.

Nori   Rice   Sake

Sesame seeds (goma)

White sesame seeds are most commonly used. You can buy them toasted (available from Asian food stores) or toast them yourself in a dry frying pan over medium heat, moving them around so that they turn golden brown and do not burn. Black sesame seeds are used as a garnish for cuttlefish and are sometimes used for sushi decoration.

Shiitake mushrooms

When buying fresh shiitake mushrooms, choose plump-looking ones with dark brown caps, cleanly tucked edges and white coloring underneath. For use in sushi, shiitake mushrooms may be parboiled, but they taste better if they have been lightly grilled. To prepare shiitake mushrooms, use a knife to score an asterisk pattern on the caps, but avoid cutting through the flesh. This ensures even cooking and

Snow peas (mange-tout)

These should be bright green, and should still be crisp after blanching. Blanch in salted, boiling water for about 30 seconds before using.

Snow pea sprouts

Available from produce vegetable stores, snow pea sprouts are sold in packets that prevent them being crushed and keep them fresh.

Soboro

A pink ingredient made from white fish, used in chirashi-zushi. You can buy it ready-made, in a jar.

Soy sauce (shoyu)

A salty sauce made from soybeans and used both as an ingredient and as a table condiment. Dark soy sauce is thicker and often less salty than light soy sauce. Low-sodium products are also available. Japanese soy is more suitable for sushi, as it is naturally fermented and less salty than Chinese soy.

Sushi vinegar (awasezu)

Sushi vinegar is a mild-tasting vinegar made from rice, as are other Japanese vinegars. It is specifically made for sushi. Other vinegars cannot be substituted, as they are too strong.

Vinegar

See sushi vinegar.

Wakame

A type of seaweed available in dried form, reconstituted under running water, used to flavor miso soup. Wakame is used in soups, salads, simmered dishes, and is finely chopped through rice. Dried wakame must be soaked before using.

Wasabi

A native Japanese plant that is found growing near clear spring water. Because of its distinctive pungent taste, it is

Shiitake mushrooms   **Shiso**   **Umeboshi**

Umeboshi

Salty pickled plums. These are available in bottles and in paste form. Keep opened bottles in the refrigerator.

Tofu

A white curd of custard-like texture made from soaking soybeans. Use the Japanese "silken" variety, which has a soft, glossy surface and a melt-in-your-mouth texture. Japanese tofu is softer and smoother than Chinese tofu. Once opened, tofu must be kept in the refrigerator, in water deep enough to cover it. Change the water at least twice a day. Stored this way, tofu will last 2 days. Slices of deep-fried tofu, known as abura-age-dofu, are used to make pouches that are stuffed with sushi rice, known as inari-zushi (see page 126). Tofu is widely available; abura-age can be found in Asian supermarkets.

often called Japanese mustard or horseradish. Wasabi roots are olive green with a bumpy skin. The best roots are 4–5 years old, 4–6 inches (10–15 cm) long, and should be fat and moist. Fresh wasabi is expensive and largely unavailable outside Japan, so powdered or paste formulations are commonly used. The powder, which is mixed with a small amount of tepid water to make a paste, is the more economical of the two. You can sometimes buy frozen grated wasabi, or you can mix Western horseradish with wasabi powder. When served as an accompaniment to sushi, wasabi is sometimes made into a decorative shape, such as a leaf. When making wasabi paste from powdered wasabi, prepare only a small quantity at a time as its potency diminishes quickly.

Fish and seafood

For health, taste, and beauty, buy the freshest fish possible for making sashimi and sushi. If you can, go to the fish markets, and always buy fish and seafood in season. Most fish can be eaten raw, but it is best to use fish that are commonly used in sashimi and sushi. Fish and seafood should be kept refrigerated until needed.

Selecting whole fish

Whenever possible, buy fish whole and fillet them at home. You can then be sure that the meat is fresh. Use the following guidelines to ensure that whole fish are fresh.

- Check that the eyes are plump, clear and bright. Avoid fish with cloudy pupils.
- The gills should be bright pink-red and look moist. If fish is not fresh, the gills are black-red.
- Overall, the coloring of the fish should be bright or lustrous.
- Stroke the fish to ensure that the flesh is firm and elastic. Stale fish are less elastic and may feel sticky.
- The fish should have a "clean" smell. Avoid ones that have a strong fishy odor.
- Mackerel should have a pointed shape to their stomachs, and the tail on both mackerel and bonito should be upright. A drooping tail shows that a fish is not fresh.

Selecting portions of fish

With bigger fish, it may be inconvenient or uneconomical to buy a whole fish, so buy fillets and smaller cuts. When buying only a portion of a fish, use the following guidelines.

- Fillets should be moist and have a good color.
- White fish should look almost transparent.
- Cut tuna flesh should have distinct stripes in it around the belly and be clear red without stripes in other parts.
- The head end of fish is more tender than the tail end.
- With most fish, the back is the most delicious part. Tuna and swordfish are exceptions, in that the tender, fatty belly area is most sought-after.

Selecting seafood

- When buying shrimp, if they are alive they should be active and of good color. If they are no longer alive, check that the stripes are distinct: they should not be blurred together.
- Touch the tentacles of squid and check that the suckers are still active. The skin around the eyes should be clear blue.
- Sea urchins should be yellow or orange, firm and not slimy.
- Live shellfish are best. When you gently open the shell, it should close by itself.

Selecting fish

To guarantee the freshness of fish, find a fish store known for having sashimi-quality fish. To determine the freshness of whole fish, make sure fish has bloodless, sparkling, crystal-clear eyes, bright pink gills, skin with a vivid color, a pleasant sea smell, and flesh that is firm and resilient to the touch. Most saltwater fish can be eaten as sushi. If using fresh-water fish, it should be filleted and sliced, then placed in iced water immediately to tighten the texture of the flesh. Alternatively, freshwater fish can be served in citrus vinaigrette.

After purchasing fish, refrigerate as soon as possible. If you have time, clean fish and fillet to maintain its freshness. Store in refrigerator no longer than 2 days.

Tuna (maguro)

Mackerel (saba)

Bonito (katsuo)
A relative of the tuna, bonito has red flesh and a strong taste. Combine it with a strong garnish such as ginger. Also known as skip jack

Cuttlefish (ika)
Look for fish with firm flesh and undamaged bodies. If cuttlefish is unavailable, substitute squid (calamari).

Garfish (sayori)
This small, slender fish has a long silver body and sweet-flavored flesh. Check that the body is firm. Also called Japanese half beak. If garfish is unavailable, substitute whiting.

John Dory (matou-dai)
The clear flesh of this fish is good for paper-thin sashimi. Lemon or other citrus juices or vinegar are recommended sauces. If John Dory is unavailable, substitute lemon sole.

King fish (buri)
This fish can be found in different sizes. The 32 lb (15 kg) size is most suitable for sashimi. In Japan, the king fish is called "shusse-uo," meaning a fish whose name and texture are changed four times as it grows. If king fish is unavailable, substitute yellowtail.

Lemon sole (hirame)
A whole lemon sole weighs about 2 lb (1 kg). Autumn and winter are the best seasons for purchasing. Also known as olive flounder or common flounder.

Mackerel (saba)
It is economical to buy mackerel whole. Its freshness diminishes rapidly, so it must be used immediately after purchase. Mackerel is usually marinated (see recipe page 199).

Ocean perch
Ocean perch is a Western fish. It has shiny fins and firm white flesh. When preparing, scale and remove skin and blanch.

Garfish (sayori)

Snapper (tai)

Salmon (shake)

The orange color of salmon is very attractive on a plate. To store, clean, then wrap in plastic and refrigerate for up 2 days. If salmon is unavailable, substitute ocean trout.

Snapper (tai)

If kept under under proper conditions, snapper can be used up to 36 hours after catching. Snapper can be enjoyed as paper-thin and as blanched sashimi.

Trevally (shimaaji)

This fish, a member of the jack family, is generally greenish on the upper half and silver on the lower. Substitute yellowtail.

Trumpeter (isake)

This fish is deep bronze in color, with white lines running along its body. It is about 12 inches (30 cm) in length. The whole fish is usable. Also called sharp-nosed tiger fish. If trumpeter is unavailable, substitute king fish

Tuna (maguro)

Tuna is one of the most popular fish for sushi because of its rich color and full-bodied flavor. Purchase only a block the size you need, and check that the flesh is firm.

Whitebait (shirauo)

The size of matchsticks, these small silvery fish resemble shards of ice. Their bones are edible.

Whiting (kisu)

The sweet-tasting, tender, fine white flesh is well suited for paper-thin sashimi. It's best to purchase a whole whiting. Fillets can also be used; be sure they do not have brown markings.

Yellowtail (aji)

Yellowtail is good for sushi and sashimi. With appropriate storage, it can be enjoyed for up to sixty hours after catching.

Preparing fish and seafood

Before cutting the fish, rinse and wipe your cutting board. Either keep a bowl of water beside you to wet your knife and then wipe it, or wipe the knife occasionally with a clean, damp cloth.

There are various methods for cutting different types of fish. The most common of these is the three-part method, or san-mai oroshi style. This is used for most fish, apart from larger flatfish and very large fish.

If you have problems holding the fish, or the bones are scratching you, use a clean kitchen glove on the hand that is holding the fish. Try not to handle the body of the fish too much as you may cause bruising. Hold the fish by its head or tail whenever possible.

Three-part method for filleting fish (san-mai oroshi style)

1 Scale fish if scaling is required. Using a sharp knife, slit belly of fish, remove viscera and rinse briefly. Avoid using too much tap water, as it will affect the taste. Lay fish down on board. Place knife behind gills and cut off head.
2 With one hand holding fish firmly, start cutting into the fillet from the (missing) head to the tail, along the back-bone of the fish, lifting the fillet away as you cut. Place first fillet aside. Turn the fish over and repeat the process.
3 Pluck or trim away any remaining bones in the fillets or around the visceral area.
4 You should now have 3 parts: 2 fillets and 1 consisting of the skeleton and the tail. Discard skeleton and tail.

Garfish filleting

Small fish like garfish are good to work with if you are first learning how to fillet. The filleting method is quite similar to the three-piece filleting method (see page 40), but is much easier.

1 Using a sharp knife, place blade behind gill and fin and cut off head. Slit belly of fish, remove viscera, and rinse fish thoroughly under running water.
2 With one hand holding fish firmly, start cutting into the fillet from the (missing) head to the tail, along the backbone of the fish, lifting the fillet away as you cut. Turn fish over and repeat process.
3 Now you have 2 fillets, and 1 piece consisting of skeleton and bones. Discard this, as it is not edible.
4 Using fingers, peel off the skin of each fillet, from (missing) head to tail.

Sushi and sashimi cutting

When cutting fish for sushi and sashimi, always cut with the knife pulling the slice toward you. The flesh should be sliced on the bias along the length of the fish or the fillet to give the best results texturally, visually and for taste.

For sashimi, there are some basic cutting techniques: a straight-down cut, an angled cut (also used for sushi), a cubic cut (for tuna), a flat cut that is then cut into fine thread-like strips, and a paper-thin-slice cut.

Any fish can be cut in these styles and eaten as sashimi, or these basic techniques can be used as a foundation for more decorative sashimi.

Angled cut for sushi and sashimi (sorigiri)

To slice fish for sushi topping, the ideal is to start with a rectangular block of fish about the width of your hand, measuring about 3 inches (7 cm) across and 1½ inches (4 cm) high. With a large fish, such as tuna, you would be able to cut a block like this from the larger block that you had bought. With other fish, such as salmon, try to cut the fish into a block, although the ends and sides may not be particularly even. With salmon or white fish, you can often cut following the existing angle of the fillet.

Measure about 1½ inches (4 cm) in from the top and slice off a triangular piece to make an angled edge to work with. (Any scraps can be used in rolled sushi.)

With your knife on a slant to match the angle of the working edge of the block, cut slices about ¼–½ inch (6 mm–1 cm) thick. The remaining piece of the block will also be triangular

This method is also used with smaller filleted fish, adjusting the knife angle to suit the fillet. With fish such as tuna, the resulting slices will be uniform and rectangular. With smaller fillets, you may have triangular edges or thinner slices. Sometimes you may need to use more than one slice for a piece of nigiri-zushi.

Sashimi cuts

Straight cut: Using a squared-off edge of filleted fish, cut ¼-inch (6-mm) slices straight down along the fish. With tuna, the slices need to be a little thicker than for some other fish because the flesh is likely to break up along the lines if the slices are thin.

Cubic cut for tuna: Slice straight down through the fish, making ½–1-inch (12 mm–2.5-cm) thick slices, then cut the slices into cubes of the same width.

Fine-strip cut for white fish or squid: Cut ¼ inch (½ cm) straight slices from the fillet. Lay each slice flat and cut them lengthwise into strips ½ inch (1 cm) wide.

Paper-thin slicing for white fish: Measure about 1½ inches (4 cm) in from the top of the block of fish and slice off a triangular piece to make an angled edge to work with. Steadily use your knife to cut paper-thin slices at an angle along the fish. With many white fish, the resulting slices are almost transparent.

Opposite page, clockwise from top left: angled cut, paper-thin slicing, straight cut.

Sushi rice

Tips for making perfect sushi rice

1 To successfully make sushi rice, choose short or medium grain rice; this has the right texture, taste and consistency to cling together without being too sticky when cooked.
2 A rice cooker is highly recommended as it produces perfect rice every time. The absorption method in a saucepan or microwave also works well, but avoid the rapid boil method.
3 Rinse rice 3–4 times before cooking to remove excess surface starch that could make the rice too sticky. Drain for 15 minutes.
4 Cool warm rice using an electric fan on lowest setting.

5 The standard rice cup provided with a rice cooker = 1 cup (5 oz/150 g) uncooked rice; 1 metric cup (8 oz/ 250 g) = about $1^{1}/_{3}$ cups (7 oz/220 g) uncooked rice. Be sure to use the same cup to measure rice and water.
6 The texture of cooked rice is a matter of taste and varies with the age and storage conditions of uncooked rice. For a softer rice texture, cook the rice with a little more water. For a firmer texture, decrease the water amount.
7 Sushi rice is cooked with slightly less water than rice served as a side dish. It is slightly firmer and chewier than plain steamed rice.

Sushi rice

3 cups (20 oz/600 g) uncooked short grain rice
3–$3^{1}/_{4}$ cups (24–27 fl oz/750–815 ml) water depending on age of rice and texture preference (see Tip number 6 above)

Sushi vinegar
8 tablespoons (3.5 fl oz/120 ml) rice vinegar
4 tablespoons sugar
$^{1}/_{2}$ teaspoon salt

Makes about 9 cups (about 3 lb/1.5 kg), depending on how densely rice was packed.

For additional flavor, add a piece of konbu or a little sake to the rice while it is cooking. For variety, add grated lemon zest, finely chopped fresh herbs, roasted nuts, toasted sesame seeds, pickled vegetables, wakame (seaweed) or finely grated fresh ginger to cooked sushi rice.

Tip for making black sushi rice
Follow the steps for white sushi rice on page 45, with the following variations: at Step 1, combine uncooked short-grain rice with 3 tablespoons of uncooked black rice. At Step 4, combine salt and vinegar, but add 1 tablespoon mirin and only 2 tablespoons sugar.

Brown sushi rice

2 cups (13 oz/400 g) uncooked short grain brown rice
$2^{3}/_{4}$–3 cups water (22–24 fl oz/685–750 ml), depending on age of rice and texture preference (see Tip number 6 above)

Sushi vinegar
$^{1}/_{4}$ cup (2 fl oz/60 ml) rice vinegar
2 tablespoons sugar
$^{1}/_{4}$ teaspoon salt

Although short grain brown rice does not cling as easily as short grain white rice, its nutty flavor and chewier texture make an interesting alternative.

Rinse brown rice once and cook as white sushi rice until most liquid is absorbed, about 30–35 minutes. Remove from heat and stand, covered, 10–15 minutes longer. Combine ingredients of sushi vinegar, stir into rice and fan to cool.

1 Put rice in a bowl, fill bowl with cold water and mix gently with hand. Drain and repeat 2–3 times until water is nearly clear.

2 Leave rice under cold running water for a few minutes.

3 Drain well for 15–30 minutes or put rice and measured water in rice cooker or saucepan and let stand for 30 minutes.

4 To make sushi vinegar: Combine vinegar, sugar and salt, stirring well until sugar dissolves. Mixture can be gently heated to dissolve sugar and make the vinegar slightly milder. Set aside until required.

5 To cook rice in a rice cooker: Measure rice. After rinsing, put rice in rice cooker and add water to the required cup measurement marked on inside of bowl in rice cooker. Cover and switch to cook. When cooker switches to keep warm, let stand with lid on to complete cooking process, about 10 minutes.

6 To cook rice in a saucepan: In a medium saucepan bring rinsed rice and water to a boil. Reduce heat and simmer, covered, on low heat until all water is absorbed, 12–15 minutes.

7 Remove from heat and let stand with lid on to complete the cooking process, 10–15 minutes. Note: Rice can also be cooked in the microwave or steamed in a bamboo steamer.

8 Spread rice out in a large, preferably flat-bottomed, nonmetallic bowl or tub

9 Using a rice paddle or wooden spoon, slice through rice at a 45 degree angle to break up any lumps, while slowly pouring sushi vinegar over rice to distribute evenly. You may not need all the vinegar.

10 Continue to slice, not stir (as it squashes the grains), lifting and turning the rice from the outside into the center

11 Fan the rice so it cools to body temperature, turning it occasionally, 5–8 minutes. Cooling gives good flavor, texture and gloss to the rice. If rice becomes too cold it hardens; do not refrigerate.

12 To stop rice from drying out, keep covered with a damp cloth while making sushi. Alternatively, keep in a nonstick surface rice cooker.

Garnishes

Cucumber curls: Thinly peel around the cucumber at 45 degrees. Reshape into a cone and fill with condiments (such as wasabi) to use as a garnish on a sushi platter.

Cucumber decoration: Slice an unpeeled cucumber about $1/4$ inch (6 mm) thick $2^1/2$ inches (6 cm) long and $3/4$ inch (2 cm) wide. Cut into an odd number of thin strips leaving $3/4$ inch (2 cm) uncut at one end. Fold every second strip down towards the middle.

Cucumber or radish cups: Slice the base off a fresh red radish or cut a piece of unpeeled cucumber about $1^1/4$ inches (3 cm) long. Make three or four 45 degree cuts downward around the radish or cucumber and discard the middle section. Use the decorative cup as a dish for condiments, such as wasabi or mustard. Soak radish cup in ice water to open the petals more. Fill with contrasting condiment color for best decoration.

Decorative leaves: Lay fresh, washed, pesticide-free camellia or lemon leaves flat and cut "D" section out from either side of central vein with a sharp knife or scalpel.

Ginger rose: Lay pieces of pickled ginger across a chopping board, each one slightly overlapping the piece next to it. Pick up the edge nearest you and roll to the other end. Stand the roll on its end and slightly open the top out so it resembles a rose. Serve with a wasabi leaf as garnish.

Lemon curls: Use a lemon zester to thinly shred and curl lemon peel for decoration.

Seasonal garnishes: Use a sprig of leaves or herbs or a small spray of blossom as a seasonal decoration on the plate, at the place settings or as a chopstick rest.

Simple leaf garnish: Arrange condiments on a fresh washed leaf—shiso, camellia, lemon—for a very simple but effective decoration.

Triangular lemon twists: Cut a slit halfway through each end of a rectangular slice of peel approximately 1 x $1/2$ inch (2.5 x 1 cm), not quite opposite each other. Trim any excess, then twist so the pieces form an open triangle. Also suitable for limes, oranges, cucumber and carrot.

Vegetable flowers: Cut a 2-inch (5-cm) piece of peeled daikon and carrot. Place on end and cut out using a knife or a decorative flower-shaped biscuit cutter. Thinly slice both inside and outside sections of both vegetables to use as an edible garnish or in soups. For a more elaborate garnish, put carrot slices in a daikon surround and daikon slices in a carrot surround. This technique can be used to cut other vegetables, such as beets (beetroot) and carrots.

Wasabi leaf: Add enough water to wasabi powder to make a soft, spreadable paste. Roll about a teaspoon of wasabi paste or fresh wasabi into a small ball. Gently flatten and shape with fingers into a leaf shape. Using a knife or toothpick, lightly mark a central vein down the middle and side veins at a 45 degree angle. Place next to a ginger rose so that guests can help themselves

Wasabi leaf

Cucumber curls   Cucumber decoration   Radish cups

Decorative leaves   Ginger rose   Lemon curls

Seasonal rosemary garnish   Simple leaf garnish   Triangular lemon twists

Thick sushi rolls
(Futomaki-zushi)

There are many variations of sushi rolls, but basically they are divided into thick sushi rolls or thin sushi rolls, depending on whether a half or whole sheet of nori (seaweed) is used. Instructions on how to roll sushi using a bamboo mat can be found on page 50.

Futomaki-zushi is thick, typically using a full-sized sheet of nori, spread evenly with a layer of vinegared rice and enclosing several fillings and sometimes a dab of wasabi. A large variety of fillings may be used, such as crisp vegetables, seafood, omelette and pickles, making it a very tasty, versatile type of sushi.

Thick rolls can be rolled in a variety of ways to make decorative patterns in the rice. Experiment with the way you lay out the ingredients and see the differing patterns that result. It is best to serve rolls as soon as they are made, because the rice inside expands and the nori tends to split. The rolls will keep for up to half an hour before serving if they are rolled in paper towel and then plastic wrap.

Step-by-step
sushi rolls

Makes 4 rolls (32 pieces)

4 sheets nori
4 cups (20 oz/600 g) sushi rice (see page 44)
2 teaspoons wasabi paste
4 strips seasoned kampyo (see page 229)
1/2 English (hothouse) cucumber, seeded and thinly sliced
4 strips thick seasoned omelette (see page 231)
4 strips pickled radish (takuan)
2 tablespoons beni-shoga
1/4 cup (2 fl oz/60 ml) Japanese soy sauce
finger bowl: water with a splash of rice vinegar

Place long side of one nori sheet lengthwise on bamboo mat about 3 slats from the edge closest to you, shiny side down. Dip both hands in finger bowl, shaking off excess. Working from one side to the other, spread one-quarter of rice evenly over nori leaving a 1-inch (2.5-cm) strip uncovered on the long side farthest from you. Gently rake fingers across grains to spread rice evenly. Build a small mound of rice along edge nearest the uncovered nori strip to help keep fillings in place.

Spread a pinch of wasabi across center of rice then layer fillings, making sure each extends completely to both ends so there will be filling in the end pieces when cut. Using your index finger and thumb, pick up edge of bamboo mat nearest you.

Place remaining fingers over fillings to hold them as you roll mat forward tightly, wrapping rice and nori around fillings. The strip of nori without rice should still be visible.

Press gently and continue rolling forward to complete roll. Gently press mat to shape and seal roll. Unroll mat and place roll on cutting board with seam on bottom.

Wipe a sharp knife with a damp cloth and cut roll in half. Pick up one half roll and turn it 180 degrees so cut ends are on the same side. Cut rolls in half, then in half again to make 8 pieces, wiping knife between cuts. Repeat for remaining rolls. Serve with remaining wasabi and soy sauce.

Filling variations
- Seasoned kampyo (see page 229), cucumber, omelette, pickled radish (takuan).
- Beni-shoga, cucumber, omelette, sliced bamboo shoots, strips seasoned tofu or tempeh.
- Cucumber, shredded carrot, red bell pepper (capsicum), avocado, toasted sesame seeds, seasoned shiitake mushrooms, scallions (shallots/spring onions).
- Tempura roll: Hot tempura vegetables, cucumber, shredded lettuce, wasabi, mayonnaise (or substitute wasabi and mayonnaise with sweet chili sauce).
- Seafood: Japanese crabmeat, sashimi tuna or salmon, denbu/oboro, or cooked shrimp (prawns).

California rolls

Makes 4 rolls (32 pieces)

4 nori sheets
3 cups (15 oz/470 g) sushi rice (see page 44)
8 teaspoons ocean trout roe or tobiko (flying fish roe)
1–2 cucumbers, cut into thin, lengthwise slices
8 jumbo shrimp (king prawns), cooked, shelled, veins and
    tails removed (see page 101)
1–2 avocados, peeled, pitted and sliced
4–8 lettuce leaves, torn or sliced (optional)

California rolls, as their name suggests, were invented in
California, although thick sushi rolls originated in the Osaka
area.

Lay 1 nori sheet on a rolling mat and put ³/₄ cup (4 oz/125 g)
sushi rice on it. Spread rice over nori sheet, leaving ³/₄ inch
(2 cm) of bare nori at far side and making a small ledge of rice
in front of this bare strip.

Spoon 2 teaspoons roe along center of rice, using back of a
spoon to spread. Lay 2 shrimp along center, with one-quarter
of cucumber strips. Lay one-quarter of avocado slices along
center. Add one-quarter of lettuce. Roll mat over once, away
from you, pressing ingredients in to keep roll firm, leaving the
³/₄-inch (2-cm) strip of nori rice-free (see page 50–51).
Covering roll (but not rice-free strip of nori), hold rolling mat in
position and press all around to make roll firm. Lift up top of
rolling mat and turn roll over a little more so that strip of nori on
far side joins other edge of nori to seal roll. Use your fingers to
make sure roll is properly closed..Roll entire roll once more, and
use finger pressure to shape roll in a circle, an oval, or a
square.

Using a sharp knife, cut each roll in half, then cut each half in
half again. Then cut each quarter in half crosswise to make a
total of 8 equal-sized pieces. Cut gently to maintain shape.

Vegetarian California rolls

Makes 4 rolls (32 pieces)

2 teaspoons wasabi paste
2 tablespoons mayonnaise
4 sheets nori
4 cups (20 oz/600 g) sushi rice (see page 44)
1 English (hothouse) cucumber, seeded and thinly sliced
1 avocado, peeled and thinly sliced
1 carrot, coarsely shredded
1 cup (2 oz/60 g) snow pea (mange-tout) sprouts, stems
   trimmed
4 shiso or small lettuce leaves, shredded (optional)
2 tablespoons gari
1/4 cup (2 fl oz/60 ml) Japanese soy sauce
finger bowl: water with a splash of rice vinegar

In a small bowl, combine wasabi and mayonnaise. Prepare rolls as for large sushi rolls (see page 50), spreading wasabi mayonnaise across the rice before adding other ingredients. Roll up using bamboo mat. Gently press mat to shape and seal roll. Unroll mat and place roll on cutting board with seam on bottom. Cut roll in half, then half again to make 8 pieces. Repeat for remaining rolls.

Filling variations
Seafood: Cooked shrimp (prawn), crabmeat, flying fish roe, sashimi tuna and salmon.

Cellophane sushi

Makes 4 rolls (32 pieces)

4 oz (125 g) dried cellophane noodles

2 teaspoons rice vinegar

1 teaspoon sugar

pinch salt

2 scallions (shallots/spring onions), green parts only, thinly
sliced

4 sheets nori

2 teaspoons wasabi paste

$1/2$ English (hothouse) cucumber, seeded and thinly
sliced, skin on

$1/2$ red bell pepper (capsicum), thinly sliced

1 small carrot, peeled, thinly sliced lengthwise

1 cup (2 oz/60 g) snow pea (mange-tout) sprouts

$1/4$ cup (2 fl oz/60 ml) miso sesame dipping sauce, ginger
sesame, or chili soy sauce, for dipping (see pages 222,
224, 225)

finger bowl: water with a splash of rice vinegar

Put noodles in a large bowl, cover with boiling water and soak until tender, 3–5 minutes. Rinse under cold water, drain well and pat dry with paper towel. Combine vinegar, sugar and salt, stirring until sugar dissolves. Mix with noodles and scallions.

Place one nori sheet lengthwise on bamboo mat about 3 slats from edge nearest you, shiny side down. Dip both hands in finger bowl, shaking off excess. Spread one-quarter of noodles evenly over nori, leaving a $1^{1}/2$-inch (4-cm) strip on farthest side uncovered. Make a hollow across center of noodles. Spread a pinch of wasabi across noodles and top with strips of cucumber, bell pepper, carrot and snow pea sprouts. Using your index finger and thumb, pick up bamboo mat, holding fillings in place with other fingers, and roll nori over noodles. Unroll mat and place roll on cutting board with seam on bottom. Wipe a sharp knife with a damp cloth and cut roll into 6 or 8 pieces, wiping knife after each cut. Repeat for remaining rolls. Serve with choice of dipping sauces.

Futomaki with kampyo, omelette, soboro and cucumber

Makes 4 rolls (32 pieces)

4 nori sheets
3 cups (15 oz/470 g) sushi rice (see page 44)
2 oz (60 g) seasoned kampyo (see page 229)
1–2 cucumbers, cut into thin slices lengthwise
shredded thin 3-egg omelette (see recipe and Tip on
   page 104)
seasoned shiitake mushrooms (see page 229)
shredded watercress, parsley or spinach leaves; bamboo
   shoots; soboro (optional)

Lay 1 nori sheet on a rolling mat and put $^3/_4$ cup (4 oz/125 g) sushi rice on it. Spread rice over nori sheet, leaving $^3/_4$ inch (2 cm) of bare nori at far side and making a small ledge of rice in front of this bare strip.

Evenly spread one-quarter of all the ingredients along center of rice. Roll mat over once, away from you, pressing ingredients in to keep roll firm, leaving the $^3/_4$-inch (2-cm) strip of nori rice-free (see pages 50–51). Covering roll (but not rice-free strip of nori), hold rolling mat in position and press all around to make roll firm. Lift up top of rolling mat and turn roll over a little more so that strip of nori on far side joins other edge of nori to seal roll. Use your fingers to make sure roll is properly closed. Roll entire roll once more, and use finger pressure to shape roll in a circle, an oval, or a square.

Using a sharp knife, cut each roll in half, then cut each half in half again. Then cut each quarter in half crosswise to make a total of 8 equal-sized pieces. Cut gently to maintain shape.

Pin wheel sushi rolls

Makes 4 rolls (32 pieces)

4 sheets nori
4 cups (20 oz/600 g) sushi rice (see page 44)
2 teaspoons wasabi paste
5–6 fillings per roll (see list below)
2 tablespoons gari
$1/4$ cup (2 fl oz/60 ml) Japanese soy sauce
finger bowl: water with a splash of rice vinegar

Make these sushi rolls the same way as large sushi rolls (see pages 50–51), except lay fillings across rice so that when rolled, ingredients and nori form a pin wheel pattern. Alternate different colored ingredients for different effects. Using the same ingredients, make inside-out rolls (see page 82) with rice on the outside. Then, sprinkle rice with toasted sesame seeds or fresh herbs.

Place short side of one nori sheet lengthwise on bamboo mat about 3 slats from edge closest to you, shiny side down. Dip both hands in finger bowl, shaking off excess. Working from one side to the other, spread one quarter of rice evenly over nori leaving a 1-inch (2.5-cm) strip on the long side farthest from you uncovered. Gently rake fingers across grains to spread rice. Spread a pinch of wasabi across center of rice. Place fillings across rice next to each other, beginning about

$3/4$ inch (2 cm) from edge nearest you and extending to within $1^1/2$ inches (4 cm) of opposite edge. Make sure fillings extend completely to each side or there will be no filling in end pieces when cut.

Using your index finger and thumb, pick up edge of bamboo mat nearest you. Roll forward straight down over first filling. Continue rolling forward to complete roll, pulling mat forward as you go so it does not get rolled in with rice. Gently press mat to shape roll. Unroll mat and place roll on cutting board with seam on bottom.

Wipe a sharp knife with a damp cloth and cut roll in half. Pick up one half roll and turn it 180 degrees so cut ends of rolls are on the same side. Cut rolls in half, then in half again to make 8 pieces, wiping knife after each cut. Repeat for remaining rolls. Serve with remaining wasabi, gari and soy sauce.

Filling variations
- Mayonnaise, cucumber, avocado, snow pea (mange-tout) sprouts, lettuce.
- Cucumber, shredded carrot, bell pepper (capsicum), avocado, snow pea (mange-tout) sprouts.
- Seasoned shiitake mushrooms (see page 229), omelette, seasoned kampyo (see page 229), blanched spinach.

Salmon and avocado roll

Makes 8 pieces

1 sheet nori
$3/4$ cup ($3^1/2$ oz/105 g) cooked sushi rice (see page 44)
pinch wasabi paste
$1/2$ medium, ripe avocado, cut in half lengthwise
2 strips of sashimi-grade salmon, each $5/8$ inch by $5/8$ inch
   by $3^1/2$ inches (13 mm by 13 mm by 9 cm)

Place nori sheet on a sushi mat, about 1 inch (2.5 cm) from edge closest to you. Wet hands and place sushi rice on nori and spread out evenly, leaving a strip of nori bare along edge farthest from you. Making a slightly raised ridge next to the bare strip will help keep filling in place. With a finger, spread a thin line of wasabi evenly across center of rice.

Lay avocado slices over wasabi. Lay salmon strips along center with avocado.

Lifting edge of mat closest to you, roll away from you, pressing on ingredients to keep them firm. Leave bare edge of nori free. With sushi mat covering the roll and bare strip still free, hold mat in position and press to make the roll firm. Lift top of sushi mat and roll so that the bare strip of nori seals the roll. Make sure the roll is completely closed.

Open mat and move the roll so one end of it is flush with one edge of the mat. Roll the mat and then pat your fingers against the end of the mat to make the end straight. Repeat with other end. Press the entire roll once more with the mat to shape it into an oval, circle or square.

Using a very sharp knife, cut the roll in half crosswise. Cut each roll in half again and then cut the quarters in half to make 8 uniform slices. Cut rolls gently so they retain their shape.

Soba noodle sushi

Makes 4 rolls (32 pieces)

8 cups (64 fl oz/2 L) water
6 oz (180 g) dried soba noodles
2 tablespoons finely sliced scallions (shallots/spring
   onions), green part only
1¹/₂ tablespoons light Japanese soy sauce
1¹/₂ tablespoons rice vinegar
1 tablespoon vegetable oil
1 teaspoon wasabi paste
2 tablespoons finely chopped gari or beni-shoga
4 sheets nori
1 English (hothouse) cucumber, seeded and finely sliced
   lengthwise, skin on
1 red bell pepper (capsicum), seeded and thinly sliced
1 carrot, thinly sliced lengthwise or grated
1 tablespoon toasted white sesame seeds
¹/₄ cup (2 fl oz/60 ml) Japanese soy sauce
finger bowl: water with a splash of rice vinegar

In a large pot over high heat, bring water to a boil. Gradually add noodles so they do not stick together. Return water to a boil then reduce heat and simmer until noodles are tender but still al dente, 8–10 minutes. Drain and rinse under cold water. Drain again and pat dry with paper towel. Combine noodles, scallions, soy sauce, vinegar, oil, wasabi and gari, adjusting seasoning to taste. Place one nori sheet lengthwise on a bamboo mat, about 3 slats from edge nearest you, shiny side down. Dip both hands in finger bowl, shaking off excess. Lay one-quarter of noodle mixture across bottom third of nori, making sure it extends completely to each end. Add one-quarter of cucumber, bell pepper and carrot strips. Using your index finger and thumb, pick up bamboo mat and, holding fillings in place with remaining fingers, roll nori over noodles. Unroll mat and place roll on cutting board with seam on bottom. Repeat for remaining rolls. Wipe a sharp knife with a damp cloth and cut roll into 8 pieces, wiping knife after each cut. Repeat for remaining rolls. Sprinkle with toasted sesame seeds and serve with soy sauce and extra gari and wasabi (if desired).

Somen noodle sushi

Makes 4 rolls (24 pieces)

4 cups (32 fl oz/1 L) water
3 oz (90 g) dried thin somen noodles
2 sheets nori
1 small carrot, thinly sliced
3 scallions (shallots/spring onions), thinly sliced
1 small red bell pepper (capsicum), thinly sliced
1 tablespoon finely chopped fresh cilantro (coriander)
  leaves
finger bowl: water with a splash of rice vinegar

For dipping sauce
¼ cup (2 fl oz/60 ml) rice vinegar
2 tablespoons Japanese soy sauce
¼ teaspoon finely chopped chili pepper
¼ teaspoon ground (minced) garlic
1 teaspoon sugar
lime or lemon juice, to taste

In a large saucepan over high heat, bring water to a boil. Add noodles and cook until tender, about 3 minutes. Drain and rinse under cold water. Drain and pat dry with paper towel.

Cut nori in half, parallel with lines marked on rough side. Place one nori sheet lengthwise on bamboo mat, 3 slats from edge closest to you, shiny side down. Place one-quarter of noodles on nori along long side nearest you. Add one-quarter of carrot slices, scallions, bell pepper and cilantro. Using your index finger and thumb, pick up bamboo mat and, holding fillings in place with other fingers, roll nori over fillings tightly. Unroll mat and place roll on cutting board with seam on bottom. Wipe a sharp knife with a damp cloth and cut roll into 6 pieces, wiping knife after each cut. Repeat with remaining rolls. Serve with dipping sauce.

To make dipping sauce: In a small bowl, combine ingredients, stirring until sugar dissolves.

Wasabi-avocado sushi canapes

Makes 2 rolls (about 28 thin pieces)

2 sheets nori

2 cups (10 oz/300 g) sushi rice (see page 44)

1 teaspoon wasabi paste

2 scallions (shallots/spring onions), green part only, thinly
  sliced

1/2 small avocado, peeled and thinly sliced

3/4 cup (1 1/2 oz/45 g) snow pea (mange-tout) sprouts,
  stems trimmed

2 tablespoons mayonnaise

These sushi rolls can be thickly or thinly sliced and used as a base to be decorated with favorite toppings. Prepare rolls as for step-by-step large sushi rolls (see pages 50–51) beginning with rice as a filling then scattering wasabi and scallions over rice. Cut roll thinly into about 1/2-inch (1-cm) pieces. Top each slice with mayonnaise, a piece of avocado and snow pea sprouts.

Yellowtail, kelp and daikon rolls

This recipe uses kelp sheets instead of nori, making a wonderful alternative to traditional sushi rolls.

Makes 4 rolls (16 pieces)

4 sheets of kelp, each trimmed into 4-inch (10-cm)
   squares, lightly boiled
4 whole yellowtail
4 paper-thin daikon slices, each 4 inches (10 cm) long
2 teaspoons tobiko (flying fish roe)
nandin leaves, for garnish
wasabi paste, for serving
Japanese soy sauce, for serving

To boil kelp: Bring a pot of water to a boil. Add kelp and cook until tender, about 15 minutes.

To slice daikon: Using a vegetable peeler, peel 4 slices of daikon, starting from top to bottom, ensuring that each slice is about 4 inches (10 cm) long.

Fillet yellowtail into three pieces (see page 40). Remove any remaining bones with tweezers. Carefully remove skin from fish with a knife. Place a kelp sheet on a board, then lay fillets on top. Roll tightly. Place a daikon slice on board, top with kelp roll, and roll tightly. Cut roll into 4 pieces. Repeat with remaining kelp, yellowtail and daikon. Divide rolls among 4 plates and garnish with nandin leaves.

Serve with wasabi and soy sauce for dipping.

Thin sushi rolls
(Hosomaki-zushi)

Small or thin sushi rolls are a simple, easy-to-eat style of sushi that is gaining in popularity as a light lunchtime food. They are made by wrapping sushi rice and ingredients in nori seaweed and shaping the rolls with a bamboo rolling mat. Usually only one type of filling is used, as the resulting roll is quite slender. With a little practice, thin sushi rolls are quite easy to make.

For making sushi rolls, a bamboo rolling mat is essential. If you try using a length of cloth or plastic wrap instead, the results are likely to be disappointing.

Judge carefully the amount of rice and filling to place in the rolls. If the rolls are over-filled, the sheets of nori are likely to break.

If you want to add more ingredients, thus making a thicker roll, you will need to lay the nori sheet vertically on the rolling mat, giving you a larger area of nori to wrap around the ingredients.

It is best to serve rolls as soon as they are made, as the rice inside expands and the nori may split. The rolls will keep for up to 30 minutes if they are rolled in a paper towel and then plastic wrap.

Sushi rolls are always served with gari and individual bowls of soy sauce for dipping. The type of garnish to serve will depend on the fillings that have been used and on personal taste. For example, white sesame seeds and shiso go particularly well with cucumber rolls.

Asparagus and sweet red pepper sushi rolls

Makes 6 rolls (36 pieces)

2 tablespoons white sesame seeds or tahini
2 teaspoons Japanese soy sauce, or to taste
2 teaspoons sugar
3 sheets nori
3 cups (15 oz/450 g) sushi rice (see page 44)
6 thin asparagus, blanched
1/3 red bell pepper (capsicum), seeded and thinly sliced
2 tablespoons gari, for garnish
1/4 cup (2 fl oz/60 ml) Japanese soy sauce, for serving

To make dressing: Place sesame seeds in a dry frying pan over
moderate heat until golden and seeds begin to jump. Grind in
a mortar and pestle to a smooth paste. Combine with soy
sauce and sugar, stirring until sugar dissolves. If mixture is too
thick, add a little water, stock or sake.

Prepare rolls as for Cucumber and Sesame Sushi Rolls (see
page 67), using sesame dressing, asparagus and red pepper
strips as fillings. Garnish with gari and serve with soy sauce.

Variations

- Umeboshi plums or plum paste and shiso leaves. Shiso can
  be used whole wrapped around plums or finely chopped and
  sprinkled on or through rice.
- Seasoned kampyo (see page 229), toasted sesame seeds,
  sprinkle of shichimi togarashi (7 chili spice).
- Seafood: Use thin strips of cucumber and sashimi tuna.
  Smoked salmon and dill mayonnaise.

Cucumber and sesame sushi rolls

Makes 6 rolls (36 pieces)

3 sheets nori
3 cups (15 oz/450 g) sushi rice (see page 44)
1 teaspoon wasabi paste
2 tablespoons toasted white sesame seeds
1 English (hothouse) or telegraph cucumber, seeded and
    thinly sliced lengthwise
1 tablespoon gari
1/4 cup (2 fl oz/60 ml) Japanese soy sauce
finger bowl: water with a splash of rice vinegar

Cut each nori sheet in half lengthwise, parallel with the lines marked on the rough side. Place one half nori sheet lengthwise on a bamboo mat about 3 slats from the edge closest to you, shiny side down. Dip both hands in finger bowl, shaking off excess. Spread one sixth of rice evenly over nori, leaving a 3/4-inch (2-cm) strip on long side farthest away uncovered. Gently rake fingers across grains to spread rice.

Build a small mound of rice along edge nearest the uncovered nori strip to help keep fillings in place.

Spread a pinch of wasabi across center of rice. Sprinkle with sesame seeds and arrange one-third of cucumber strips, making sure they extend completely to each end. Using your index finger and thumb, pick up edge of mat nearest you. Place remaining fingers over fillings to hold them in as you roll forward, tightly wrapping rice and nori around fillings. The strip of nori without rice should still be visible.

Press gently and continue rolling forward to complete roll. Gently press mat to shape and seal roll. Unroll mat and place roll on chopping board with seam on bottom. Wipe a sharp knife with a damp cloth and cut roll in half. Pick up one half roll and turn it 180 degrees so cut ends of rolls are on the same side. Cut rolls to make 6 pieces, wiping knife between cuts. Repeat for remaining rolls. Serve with remaining wasabi, gari and soy sauce.

Cuttlefish rolls

Makes 12 pieces

1 nori sheet
4 cuttlefish
4 okra
12 shiso leaves
4 carrot strips, each 4 inches (10 cm) long and 3 inches
   (7.5 cm) wide
4 daikon strips, each 4 inches (10 cm) long and 3 inches
   (7.5 cm) wide
wasabi paste, for serving
Japanese soy sauce, for serving

Cut nori sheet into quarters and set aside. Clean cuttlefish (see page 69). Place knife blade on edge of fillet and slice in half, without cutting through. Open up cuttlefish and lay 1 piece nori on right side. Trim ends of each okra and place 1 okra on left edge of nori sheet (closest to center) of opened fillet. Fold left side right over, then tightly roll up. Cut into 3 pieces.

Arrange shiso leaves on a plate and top with cuttlefish rolls. Holding 1 carrot strip and 1 daikon strip, tie together to form knot in center. Place on plate. Repeat for remaining servings.

Serve with wasabi and soy sauce for dipping.

Variation
Buy okra that is young and tender, but for a substitute try salmon slices, tuna slices, pickled ginger or sliced cucumber.

Cleaning and working with cuttlefish

Cuttlefish have ink sacs and can therefore be messy to clean. As you work, be careful not to break the sac and release the ink.

Cuttlefish with a strong smell or an unusually slimy surface should not be used for sashimi. If cuttlefish are unavailable, squid (calamari) can be substituted.

1 Holding cuttlefish head with one hand, gently pull out shell with the other hand.

2 Gently pull out tentacles and entrails, being careful not to break the ink sac. Rinse mantle under running cold water. The tentacles can also be used for sashimi; cut them off below the eyes and remove beak. Cut tentacles into bite-sized pieces. Pour boiling water over them to blanch.

3 Slit the edge only halfway on the inside of the mantle. With a firm hold, pull the skin from the edge of the fillet you have cut open. Using a cloth makes skinning easier

4 Slice cuttlefish fillet in half, stopping just at the edge (leave 1 cm of joined flesh). Gently open fillet, using the blade carefully.

5 Trim off top and bottom of an okra. Prepare a nori sheet the width of one side of the opened cuttlefish fillet. Lay nori sheet on one half of the fillet and place okra in the center of the fold.

6 Wrap cuttlefish around okra and nori to form a cylindrical shape.

Korean kimchi rolls

Makes 8 pieces

1 teaspoon canola oil
3 oz (90 g) topside steak, thinly sliced
2 tablespoons Korean barbecue sauce
1 cup (5 oz/150 g) sushi rice (see page 44)
2 Chinese (napa) cabbage kimchi leaves
2 fresh chives
2 tablespoons white sesame seeds

Heat a heavy frying pan over high heat and add oil. Reduce heat to medium, add steak slices and cook until heated through. Add barbecue sauce and cook for 1 minute. Set aside on a plate until cool.

Cover a sushi mat with plastic wrap. Lay kimchi leaves horizontally on plastic, beginning at end closest to you. With wet fingers, spread rice over kimchi, leaving uncovered a 3/4-inch (2-cm) strip at end farthest from you. Cover rice with beef and arrange chives in center. Roll up tightly, then unroll mat, remove plastic, and transfer roll to a cutting board. Wipe a sharp knife with a damp towel and cut each roll in half, then cut each half in half again, wiping knife after each cut. Repeat with remaining ingredients.

Holding each piece with your fingers, dip into sesame seeds on a plate to coat kimchi. Arrange pieces on serving plates and serve.

Natto rolls

Makes 4 rolls (24 pieces)

2 sheets nori
1 cup (5 oz/155 g) sushi rice (see page 44)
6 tablespoons natto (fermented soybeans)
5 shiso leaves, finely chopped
pinch bonito flakes

Take one nori sheet. Cut in half lengthwise, then cut $^3/_4$ inch (2 cm) from bottom of each sheet. You should have 2 sheets, each about 4 x 6$^1/_2$ inches (10 x 16.5 cm). Repeat, cutting remaining nori sheets.

Place a nori sheet lengthwise on a bamboo mat, shiny side down.

Position nori sheet about 1 inch (2.5 cm) from edge of mat closest to you, and leave some space on each side of nori sheet.

Wet your hands and take a golf ball–sized handful of sushi rice. Gently squeeze rice into an oblong ball and put on center

left of nori sheet. Then use your fingers to squeeze rice into a log along center of nori. Spread one-quarter of natto along length of rice, and top with one-quarter of shiso leaves and bonito flakes. Tightly roll mat until it covers rice and near side and far sides of rice join at ridge, leaving a strip of nori rice-free. Lift up top of rolling mat and turn roll over a little more so that strip of nori on far side joins other edge of nori to seal roll. Use your fingers to make sure roll is properly closed. Roll entire roll once more, exerting gentle pressure.

Slice roll in half, then cut both rolls twice to give 6 equal-sized pieces. Repeat with remaining ingredients.

Nori tuna rolls

Makes 4

10 oz (300 g) tuna block
4 nori sheets, halved
4 beet (beetroot) flowers (see page 46)
1³/₄ oz (50 g) shredded daikon radish
1³/₄ oz (50 g) shredded beet (beetroot)
8 cucumber leaves
wasabi paste, for serving
Japanese soy sauce, for serving

Cut tuna into cylinders 1 inch (2.5 cm) in diameter and 4 inches (10 cm) long.

Lay a halved nori sheet on board and top with 1 tuna slice. Roll up tightly using both hands. Repeat with remaining tuna slices and nori sheets. Cut each roll into 4 pieces. Divide daikon among 4 bowls. Place 4 rolls in each bowl. Garnish with beet flower and cucumber leaves. Serve with wasabi and soy sauce for dipping.

Tip
When slicing rolled tuna on a board, keep the board dry, or nori will become soggy. Salmon may be substituted for tuna.

Pickled plum and brown rice sushi rolls

Makes 6 rolls (36 pieces)

1 tablespoon vegetable oil
2 carrots, peeled and cut lengthwise into thin strips
1 clove garlic, ground (minced)
1 teaspoon peeled and grated fresh ginger
2 eggs, lightly beaten
1 tablespoon Japanese soy sauce
1 tablespoon umeboshi plum paste
1 tablespoon rice vinegar
4 sheets nori
4 cups (20 oz/625 g) brown sushi rice (see recipe page 44)
4 scallions (shallots/spring onions), green parts only
1/4 cup (2 fl oz/60 ml) Japanese soy sauce
finger bowl: water with a splash of rice vinegar

Heat oil in frying pan over moderate heat and sauté carrot, garlic and ginger until carrots are just cooked, about 2 minutes. Remove from pan. Combine eggs and tablespoon of soy sauce and spread thinly over frying pan. Cook until just set,

about 45 seconds. Turn over and cook about 20 seconds longer. Remove from pan and slice into thin strips. Combine plum paste and vinegar and gently fold into rice.

Cut each nori sheet in half lengthwise, parallel with the lines marked on the rough side. Place one half nori sheet lengthwise on bamboo mat, about 3 slats from edge closest to you, shiny side down. Dip both hands in finger bowl, shaking off excess. Spread one-sixth of rice evenly over nori, leaving a small strip on long side farthest away from you uncovered. Make an indentation across rice and put one-sixth of carrots, egg and one scallion evenly from one side of rice to the other. Using your index finger and thumb, pick up edge of bamboo mat nearest you. Place remaining fingers over fillings to hold them as you roll mat forward, tightly wrapping rice and nori around fillings. The strip of nori without rice should still be visible. Press firmly and continue rolling forward to complete roll. Gently press mat to shape roll. Unroll mat and place roll on cutting board with seam on bottom. Wipe a knife with a damp cloth and cut roll into 6 pieces, wiping knife between cuts. Repeat with remaining rolls. Serve with soy sauce.

Thin sushi rolls **(Hosomaki-zushi)**   **73**

Radish and kampyo rolls

Makes 6 rolls (36 pieces)

3 sheets nori
3 cups (15 oz/450 g) sushi rice (see page 44)
6 strips pickled radish (takuan), 1/2 inch x 1/2 inch x
   71/4 inches (1 cm x 1 cm x 18.5 cm)
6 pieces seasoned kampyo (see page 229)
1 teaspoon wasabi paste
1 tablespoon gari
1/4 cup (2 fl oz/60 ml) Japanese soy sauce
finger bowl: water with a splash of rice vinegar

Cut each nori sheet in half lengthwise, parallel with the lines
marked on the rough side. Place one half nori sheet lengthwise
on a bamboo mat about 3 slats from the edge closest to you,
shiny side down. Dip both hands in finger bowl, shaking off
excess. Spread one-sixth of rice evenly over nori, leaving a
3/4-inch (2-cm) strip on long side farthest away from you
uncovered. Gently rake fingers across grains to spread rice.

Build a small mound of rice along edge nearest the
uncovered nori strip to help keep fillings in place.

Arrange one strip pickled radish and kampyo per roll, making
sure they extend completely to each end. Using your index
finger and thumb, pick up edge of mat nearest you. Place
remaining fingers over fillings to hold them in as you roll
forward, tightly wrapping rice and nori around fillings. The strip
of nori without rice should still be visible.

Press gently and continue rolling forward to complete roll.
Gently press mat to shape and seal roll. Unroll mat and place
roll on chopping board with seam on bottom. Wipe a sharp
knife with a damp cloth and cut roll in half. Pick up one half roll
and turn it 180 degrees so cut ends of rolls are on the same
side. Cut rolls to make 6 pieces, wiping knife between cuts.
Repeat for remaining rolls. Serve with wasabi (note:
traditionally, wasabi is not used with pickled vegetables, but
served on the side for guests to add if desired), gari and soy
sauce.

Step-by-step shrimp tempura

Makes 8 pieces

8 medium shrimp (prawns), shelled and deveined (tails intact)

1 tablespoon katakuri starch (Japanese starch) or cornstarch (cornflour) for coating ingredients

1 cup (8 fl oz/250 ml) cold water

1 cup (5 oz/150 g) tempura flour (available from Asian markets)

canola oil for deep-frying

a few drops Asian sesame oil

1 Coat shrimp with katakuri starch and set aside. Mix equal amounts of cold water and tempura flour with chopsticks or a fork.

2 Fill a tempura pan, or deep-fryer one-third full with canola oil and add sesame oil. Heat over medium-high heat to 365°F (185°C), or until a small amount of tempura batter dropped into oil rises quickly to the surface, about 1 second.

3 Dip coated food into tempura batter and place it gently into oil. Deep-fry until it is golden brown, turning occasionally.

4 Using saibashi (or cooking chopsticks), remove tempura from oil and drain on wire rack for 30 seconds; then transfer to paper towels.

Tip

Tempura is best eaten as soon as it is cooked. However, if you are using tempura as an ingredient in sushi, you should let it cool first.

Shrimp tempura rolls with basil

Makes 8 pieces

Thai basil sauce
1 tablespoon rice vinegar
1 teaspoon fish sauce
leaves from 2 Thai basil sprigs, finely chopped
1 teaspoon packed brown sugar

1 nori sheet, halved
2 cups (10 oz/300 g) sushi rice (see page 44)
4 cooked shrimp tempura (page 76)
4 fresh Thai basil leaves
1 hard-boiled egg yolk, sieved (egg mimosa)

To make Thai basil sauce: Combine all ingredients in a bowl and mix well. Set aside.

Arrange one half sheet of nori, shiny side down, on a sushi mat. With wet fingers, spread half sushi rice evenly over nori, leaving uncovered a ³/4-inch (2-cm) strip of nori on side farthest from you. Place 2 shrimp tempura over rice, allowing a tail to poke out at each end of nori. Top with 2 Thai basil leaves and roll following instructions on pages 50–51. If nori is too dry to seal, wet edge and press edge to roll with mat.

To make egg mimosa: Place a fresh egg in a pot of water. Bring water to a boil and simmer for 15 minutes until egg is hard-boiled. Remove egg shell under running water and when egg is chilled, remove egg white. Place egg yolk in a sieve. Pressing with a teaspoon, sieve into a small bowl

Unroll mat, and transfer roll to a cutting board. Wipe a sharp knife with a damp towel and cut each roll into 4 pieces, wiping knife after each cut. Repeat with remaining ingredients. Arrange pieces on plates and sprinkle sieved egg yolk over shrimp tails. Serve with Thai basil sauce.

Tip

Egg mimosa is used for sprinkling or a decoration such as the stamen in a carved radish flower.

Small rolls with celery, pastrami and pâté

Makes 8 pieces

$^{1}/_{2}$ sheet nori
1 cup (5 oz/150 g) sushi rice (see page 44)
1 teaspoon chicken liver pâté
$^{1}/_{2}$ teaspoon chili paste
1 slice pastrami
$^{1}/_{2}$ celery stick, trimmed and thinly sliced lengthwise
Japanese soy sauce, for serving

Place nori on a sushi mat, shiny side down. With wet hands, spread rice over nori. With your index finger, smear pâté and chili paste in a line down center of rice. Top with pastrami and celery. Roll tightly following instructions on pages 50–51. Unroll mat and transfer roll to a cutting board. Wipe a sharp knife with a damp towel. Cut roll in half, then cut both rolls in half again, and in half again, to make a total of 8 pieces. Wipe knife after each cut. Serve with soy sauce.

Spinach brown rice sushi rolls with miso sesame

Makes 4 rolls (24 pieces)

5 oz (150 g) spinach leaves, blanched and drained well
½ teaspoon Japanese soy sauce
2 scallions (shallots/spring onions), green part only, finely chopped
1 tablespoon toasted white sesame seeds
2 sheets nori
2 cups (10 oz/300 g) brown sushi rice (see page 44)
miso sesame sauce (see page 225)
finger bowl: water with a splash of rice vinegar

Chop spinach leaves finely and sprinkle with soy sauce. Cut each piece nori in half lengthwise, parallel with lines marked on the rough side.

Fold scallions and sesame seeds into rice until evenly distributed. Place one half nori sheet lengthwise on bamboo mat, about 3 slats from edge closest to you, shiny side down. Dip both hands in finger bowl, shaking off excess. Spread one-quarter of rice evenly over nori, leaving a ¾-inch (2-cm) strip

uncovered on long side farthest from you. Carefully make a lengthwise groove in middle of rice. Add a layer of spinach, making sure it extends evenly to each end. Using your index finger and thumb, pick up edge of the bamboo mat nearest you. Place remaining fingers over fillings to hold them as you roll mat forward, tightly wrapping rice and nori around fillings. The strip of nori without rice should still be visible.

Press firmly and continue rolling forward to complete roll. Gently press mat to shape roll. Unroll mat and place roll on cutting board with seam on bottom. Wipe a knife with a damp cloth and cut roll into 6 pieces, wiping knife with each cut. Repeat with remaining roll. Serve with miso sesame sauce.

Tuna rolls

Makes 10 rolls (60 pieces)

5 nori sheets
2 cups (10 oz/315 g) sushi rice (see page 44)
pinch wasabi paste
10 strips tuna, $1/4$ x $1/2$ x 3 inches (6 mm x 12 mm x 7.5 cm)
   (see pages 42–43)

Take one nori sheet. Cut in half lengthwise, then cut $3/4$ inch (2 cm) from bottom of each sheet. You should have 2 sheets, each about 4 x $6^1/2$ inches (10 x 16.5 cm). Repeat with remaining nori sheets.

Place a nori sheet lengthwise on a bamboo rolling mat, shiny side down.

Position nori sheet about 1 inch (2.5 cm) from edge of mat closest to you. Leave some space on each side of nori sheet.

Wet your hands and take a golf ball-sized handful of sushi rice. Gently squeeze rice into an oblong ball and put on center left of nori sheet. Then use your fingers to squeeze rice into a log along center of nori.

Take a dab of wasabi on your finger and wipe from left to right across center of rice. Place tuna strips along center of rice, over the wasabi. Place fingers flat over tuna strips to hold them in place, then use your thumbs to lift up edge of bamboo rolling mat closest to you. Roll up mat (see pages 50–51 for instructions) and seal nori strip. Slice roll in half, then cut both rolls twice to give 6 equal-sized pieces. Repeat with remaining ingredients.

Inside-out sushi rolls
(Uramaki-zushi)

As this name suggests, the rice is on the outside of the roll rather than inside. Sometimes the rice may be decorated with tobiko (flying fish roe), which can be orange, green or golden in color; toasted white or black sesame seeds; or tempura flakes. This decorative style of sushi shows a chef's creativity. Having the roe on the outside of the roll results in the delightful effect of the roe popping as it touches your tongue. The step-by-step instructions that follow show how easy it is to make uramaki-zushi.

Step-by-step
inside-out sushi rolls

Makes 4 rolls (32 pieces)

4 nori sheets

3 cups (15 oz/470 g) sushi rice (see page 44)

8 teaspoons ocean trout roe or tobiko (flying fish roe)

1–2 cucumbers, cut into thin, lengthwise slices

1–2 avocados, peeled, pitted and sliced

8 jumbo shrimp (king prawns), cooked, shelled, veins and
  tails removed (see page 101)

4–8 lettuce leaves, torn or sliced (optional)

1 Cover a rolling mat with a sheet of plastic wrap, folding it over edges and attaching it to back of mat. Turn mat over so plastic-covered side is facing down. Lay 1 nori sheet on rolling mat. Use about $3/4$ cup (4 oz/125 g) rice to cover nori sheet, starting with a ball of rice at bottom and then spreading it out. Cover nori with rice right up to edges. Spread about 2 heaped teaspoons roe over rice, using the back of a teaspoon.

2 Pick up rice-covered nori by corners, quickly turn it over and place upside down on bamboo rolling mat.

3 Add lettuce, if desired. Place sliced cucumber along center of nori. Add avocado, then shrimp. With your hands held over base of mat and pressing in on ingredients with your fingers as you go, roll mat over ingredients, leaving $3/4$ inch (2 cm) of nori visible at far end of nori end of roll.

4 Press gently to mold roll together. Lift up mat, roll back a little, then roll forward to join nori edges. Use gentle pressure to firm and mold completed roll into shape, either round, oval or square.

5 Using a sharp knife, cut each roll in half, then cut two halves in half again. Then cut four quarters in half to make 8 equal-sized pieces. Cut gently to maintain shape.

California rolls with crabmeat and avocado

Makes 8 pieces

1¹⁄₄ nori sheets
¹⁄₂ avocado, pitted, peeled, and cut into strips, each
   ¹⁄₂-inch (1-cm) thick
1 cup (5 oz/150 g) sushi rice (see page 44)
1 tablespoon golden tobiko (flying fish roe)
1 tablespoon orange tobiko (flying fish roe)
1 tablespoon wasabi tobiko
¹⁄₄ English (hothouse) cucumber, cut lengthwise then into
   strips, each ¹⁄₄ inch (6 mm) thick
2 sticks crabmeat (pressed crabmeat)

Place quartered nori sheet on a dry work surface, shiny side down, and place a strip of avocado in center of nori. Roll and set aside.

To make an inside-out sushi roll, place a whole nori sheet on a bamboo sushi mat, glossy side down, and spread sushi rice evenly over it. Using a teaspoon, spread golden, orange, and wasabi tobiko to create a striped pattern. Cut plastic wrap the same size as sushi mat and cover rice with mat. Pick up mat, place a hand over plastic wrap, and carefully turn over so nori is on top. Place back on mat about 3 slats from edge closest to you.

Place 1 slice avocado, 1 slice cucumber and 1 crabstick in center of nori. Using your index finger and thumb, pick up edge of sushi mat and plastic wrap nearest to you. Place remaining fingers over fillings to hold them as you roll mat forward tightly, wrapping rice and nori around fillings. Press gently and continue rolling forward to complete roll. Gently press mat to shape and seal roll. Unroll mat and transfer roll to a cutting board.

Wipe a sharp knife with a damp towel. Cut roll in half and cut the halves in half again; then cut each quarter in half to make 8 equal pieces, wiping knife after each cut. Finally, gently remove plastic wrap from each piece.

Cajun-style spicy rolls

Makes 8 pieces

4 smoked salmon slices
1 tablespoon cream cheese
1/4 teaspoon Cajun spice
1 cup (5 oz/150 g) sushi rice (see page 44)
6 green beans, blanched
1 teaspoon shiso (Japanese basil) powder

Cover a sushi mat with plastic wrap. Lay salmon slices horizontally across plastic from edge closest to you. Spread cream cheese across center and sprinkle with Cajun spice. With wet fingers, spread sushi rice over salmon slices, leaving 3/4 inch (2 cm) uncovered. Place green beans in a straight line. Roll up very tightly following instructions on page 84.

Unroll mat and transfer roll to a cutting board. Wipe a sharp knife with a damp towel, cut each roll in half, then cut each half into 4 pieces, wiping knife after each cut. Remove plastic from rolls.

Holding 1 piece, dip seam side into shiso powder. Arrange on serving plates. Repeat with remaining ingredients.

Golden rolls

Makes 8 pieces

¹/₂ cup (4 fl oz/125 ml) water
¹/₂ cup (2¹/₂ oz/75 g) tempura flour
canola oil for deep-frying
a few drops Asian sesame oil
1 nori sheet
1 cup (5 oz/150 g) sushi rice (see page 44)
4 slices smoked salmon
¹/₂ teaspoon wasabi paste
¹/₂ mango, cut into ¹/₄-inch (6-mm) thick strips and peeled
¹/₂ avocado, pitted, peeled and cut into each ¹/₄-inch (6-mm)
    thick strips

To make tempura flakes, gently stir water and tempura flour together in a bowl until just mixed. Fill a tempura pan or deep-fryer one-third full with canola oil. Add sesame oil. Heat over medium-high heat to 365°F (185°C), or until a drop of batter rises to the surface quickly (about 1 second). Using chopsticks or a fork, drop tempura batter into oil. Using a pair of dry chopsticks, divide flakes into small pieces as soon as they are dropped into oil. Fry until golden and crisp. Using a wire-mesh skimmer, remove to drain on a wire rack or paper towels, then transfer to paper towels and set aside.

Follow the step-by-step instructions on page 84, substituting the filling ingredients as follows. Once rice and nori are turned over, place salmon slices in center of nori. Then, using your index finger, smear with wasabi. Place 3 strips of mango on top, then top with avocado. Roll up firmly as per step-by-step instructions.

Wipe a sharp knife with a damp cloth and cut roll in half. Cut each half in half twice more to make 8 pieces, wiping knife after each cut. Gently remove plastic from rolls. Gently dip the outside of each roll into tempura flakes to give roll its golden color. It is better to add flakes to individual rolls, as flakes can become squashed during cutting.

Indonesian-flavored coconut rolls

Makes 12 pieces

1 cup (5 oz/150 g) sushi rice (see page 44)
1 tablespoon peanut sate (or satay) sauce
1 can coconut meat, drained
1 sheet nori, halved
chili (sambal) paste for serving

Cover a sushi mat with plastic wrap. Place a half sheet of nori over plastic, shiny side down, and, with wet fingers, spread half of sushi rice over nori. Holding surface of rice with one hand, turn over rice and nori, placing rice on plastic. Using your index finger, smear nori with sate sauce. Place 4 pieces coconut meat in center. Roll tightly, following instructions on page 84.

Unroll mat, remove plastic, and transfer roll to a cutting board. Wipe a sharp knife with a damp towel and cut roll in half; then cut each half into 3 pieces, wiping knife after each cut. Repeat with remaining ingredients. Serve with chili paste.

Tip
Unshredded preserved coconut meat is sold in tins or bottles. This milky-colored coconut meat has a light, fruity taste. Available from large supermarkets or Asian markets.

Kampyo and snow pea rolls

Makes 4 rolls (32 pieces)

2 sheets nori
3 cups (15 oz/500 g) sushi rice (see page 44)
1 tablespoon combined toasted black and white sesame
    seeds
1–2 tablespoons wasabi paste
1/2 English (hothouse) or telegraph cucumber, seeded and
    thinly sliced
4 strips seasoned kampyo (see page 229)
2 tablespoons beni-shoga
8 snow peas (mange-tout), blanched and thinly sliced
1/2 red bell pepper (capsicum), seeded and thinly sliced
1/4 cup (2 fl oz/60 ml) Japanese soy sauce
finger bowl: water with a splash of rice vinegar

Cut each piece of nori in half lengthwise, parallel with lines
marked on rough side. Place one half nori sheet on a bamboo
mat, along the long side of the mat nearest you. Dip both

hands in finger bowl, shaking off excess. Spread one-quarter
of rice evenly over nori. Gently rake fingers across grains to
spread rice. Sprinkle rice with mixed sesame seeds and cover
with a large sheet of plastic wrap.

Pick up mat, carefully turn over so nori is on top and place
back on mat, about 3 slats from edge closest to you. Spread a
pinch of wasabi and selection of fillings across center of nori.
Make sure fillings extend completely to each end. Using your
index finger and thumb, pick up edge of bamboo mat and
plastic wrap nearest you. Place remaining fingers over fillings to
hold them as you roll mat forward tightly, wrapping rice and
nori around fillings.

Roll up firmly following instructions on page 84. Wipe a sharp
knife with a damp cloth and cut roll in half. Cut each half in half
twice more to make 8 pieces, wiping knife after each cut.
Repeat with remaining roll. Serve with remaining wasabi and
soy sauce.

Omelette sushi rolls

Makes 2 rolls (16 pieces)

5 seasoned shiitake mushrooms (see page 229), finely
 chopped
1 seasoned carrot (see page 229), peeled and julienned
2 seasoned tofu, thinly sliced (see page 128)
2 cups (10 oz/315 g) sushi rice (see page 44)
2 thin seasoned omelettes (see page 231)
2 sheets nori
1 English (hothouse) cucumber, seeded and thinly sliced
 lengthwise
1/4 cup Japanese soy sauce, for serving
2 tablespoons gari, for serving

In a bowl, combine seasoned shiitake, seasoned carrot,
seasoned tofu and rice, mixing well.

Cover a bamboo mat with a plastic wrap. Lay one omelette
on plastic and cover with a sheet of nori. Spread nori with rice
mixture, leaving a 1-inch (2.5-cm) strip on long side farthest
away uncovered. Lay half cucumber strips across rice, making
sure they extend to each end. Pick up mat and plastic with
index finger and thumb, holding cucumber in place with
remaining fingers, and roll and seal nori around cucumber.
Unroll mat and plastic. Place roll on cutting board with seam
on bottom. Wipe a sharp knife with a damp cloth and cut roll
into 8 pieces, wiping knife before each cut. Repeat for
remaining roll. Serve with soy sauce and gari.

Variations
- Use nori half sheets to make thin rolls.
- Substitute blanched spinach or green beans for cucumber,
 and tempeh for seasoned tofu.

Smoked salmon and asparagus with cream cheese

Makes 8 pieces

1 nori sheet
1 cup (5 oz/150 g) sushi rice (see page 44)
1 teaspoon wasabi paste
2 tablespoons cream cheese
4 slices smoked salmon
4 asparagus spears, blanched and chilled
4 fresh dill sprigs, minced
Japanese soy sauce, for serving

Cover a sushi mat with plastic wrap. Place nori on plastic, shiny side down, and, with wet fingers, spread sushi rice over nori, leaving uncovered a 3/4-inch (2-cm) strip of nori on side farthest from you. Holding surface of rice with one hand, turn over rice and nori so that rice is on plastic and nori is on top. Return to mat. Using your index finger, smear wasabi and cream cheese over nori. Arrange 2 salmon slices and 2 asparagus spears in center, allowing asparagus to poke out of nori at both ends. Roll sushi following instructions on pages 84. Make sure fillings are enclosed but leave one-fourth of nori visible at end farthest from you. Lift up mat and roll forward to join nori edges. Press gently to form into a square shape.

Unroll mat, remove plastic, and transfer roll to a cutting board. Wipe a sharp knife with a damp cloth, cut roll in half, then cut each half into 4 pieces, wiping knife after each cut. Coat rolls with dill. Place rolls on plates and serve with soy sauce.

Thai-flavored papaya and vegetable rolls

Makes 8 pieces

¹/₄ English (hothouse) cucumber, seeded and julienned
¹/₄ carrot, peeled and julienned
¹/₄ papaya (cut lengthwise), peeled and seeded
³/₄ sheet nori
1 cup (5 oz/150 g) sushi rice (see page 44)
2 fresh Thai basil leaves
2 tablespoons green curry paste

Cut cucumber into strips, each ¹/₄ inch (6 mm) thick. Cut carrot and papaya into strips the same size. Set aside on a plate.

Cover a sushi mat with plastic wrap. Place nori over plastic, glossy side down, and, with wet fingers, spread sushi rice over nori. Holding surface of rice with one hand, turn over rice and nori, placing rice on plastic. Arrange cucumber, carrot, and papaya strips and basil leaves in center. Roll tightly, following instructions on page 84.

Unroll mat, remove plastic, and transfer roll to a cutting board. Wipe a sharp knife with a damp towel and cut roll in half. Cut rolls in half, then cut each piece again, wiping knife after each cut.

Arrange pieces on plates and spoon curry paste alongside.

Topped rice sushi
(nigiri-zushi)

Nigiri-zushi is the type of sushi most often made in sushi bars. In Japanese, nigiri means "squeeze." Nigiri-zushi are made by gently squeezing together bite-sized pieces of fish (or other foods) and small balls of sushi rice.

As your guide to size, remember that this style of sushi is best eaten in a single mouthful, so for each piece use a ball of rice the size of a golf ball and enough topping to cover it. Use a moderate amount of wasabi for richer, more oily fish such as tuna and salmon, and less for mild-tasting seafood such as shrimp (prawns), squid and octopus.

There are three or four commonly used methods for making nigiri-zushi but we recommend the tategaeshi style (shown on following pages) as it gives professional results and, with a little practice, is easy to master. Once you have mastered the method and tried the various recipes provided, you can use your skills to create your own style of nigiri-zushi.

Step-by-step
Topped rice sushi

In order to make it easy to handle sushi rice and topping, prepare a bowl of tezu (half water, half sushi vinegar) and have it alongside you as you work. To wet your hands to the right extent, use your right index finger (if you are right-handed) to wipe tezu on left-hand palm in a circular motion, then clap your right fist over your left hand and wipe the water off your fingers so your hands are just moist. Also have beside you a small bowl of wasabi.

For this easy at-home method, do not use slice of fish at first. When rice ball is well shaped, then add fish. You will need a little pressure to join fish to rice ball.

1 With moist hands, pick up a piece of fish and hold it in your left hand hanging between thumb and index finger. Pick up a golf ball-sized ball of rice with your right hand. Gently squeeze rice in your right hand to form a rectangular block with rounded edges and sides.

2 Lay fish piece flat in your left hand, across middle joints of your fingers.

Use your right-hand index finger to spread a dab of wasabi along length of fish.

3 Bringing your right hand over on top, place rice on top of fish.

Gently use your left thumb to press down on top of rice in middle, making a slight depression in rice.

4 Still holding your thumb to rice, turn your left hand over slowly and carefully from elbow.

5 With your right hand under your left, use your right-hand thumb and index finger to hold piece (along sides of rice).

6 Quickly turn your left hand over again so it is under your right hand (palm facing upwards) and place sushi piece back into your left hand (across middle joints of fingers). With your right hand sideways (not above fish piece), use your right-hand index finger and thumb to hold and press sides of rice gently.

7 To form sushi, you will now use three actions together:
a) Keeping your left hand relaxed and fingers slightly tilted down, your fingers will wrap upwards to hold and press sushi (which will then sit straight if you have tilted your hand down).

7 **b)** Your left-hand thumb will hold and press end of log of rice.
c) Hold your right-hand index and middle fingers straight and together and use them to gently press down along top of fish.

All these steps should be done in one quick, gentle pressing action, which is then gently released.

8 Hold your right hand over top of sushi piece and use your index and middle fingers on far side and your thumb on near side to pick up and turn sushi piece around in your left hand.

9 Repeat previous step, where you quickly pressed sushi with left thumb, left fingers and right-hand index and middle fingers.

10 You should now have a well-formed piece of sushi. If it is still not correctly formed, you may turn the piece around once more and press again. Traditionally, as a final step, the chef uses his right-hand index finger to quickly wipe along top of fish, to make fish look shiny.

Bite-sized sushi molds

Another method of creating nigiri-zushi-style sushi is to use molds. Look for molds especially designed for sushi or Japanese rice balls. Cheap alternatives are: cookie or scone cutters, ice cream scoops, ice cube trays, mini cup-cake molds, small cups and jelly molds.

Makes about 16 pieces

3 cups (15 oz/450 g) sushi rice (see page 44)
2 tablespoons white sesame seeds, toasted
1/2 cup seasoned shiitake mushrooms (see page 229)
4 seasoned kampyo (see page 229)
4 scallions (shallots/spring onions), green parts only, blanched
1 thin seasoned omelette (see page 231), cut into 1/2-inch (1-cm) strips
1/2 red bell pepper (capsicum), seeded and thinly sliced
1 English (hothouse) cucumber, seeded and thinly sliced lengthwise
1 sheet nori

1/3 cup (3 fl oz/90 ml) Japanese soy sauce
finger bowl: water with a splash of rice vinegar

In a large bowl, combine rice, sesame seeds and shiitake. Line a sushi mold or loaf cake tin, 8 inches x 3 1/2 inches (20 cm x 9 cm) with plastic wrap, allowing excess to fold over the sides. Arrange alternate strips of kampyo, scallion, omelette, bell pepper and cucumber decoratively as the base. Dip both hands in finger bowl, shaking off excess. Spread a thin layer of sushi rice over vegetables, being careful not to disturb vegetable arrangement. Fold nori sheet in half, not parallel with lines marked on rough side. Lay one half sheet of nori on top of rice. Cover nori completely with another thin layer of rice. Press down gently with fingers or back of a spoon. Lay other half sheet of nori on rice. Set a plate on mold, making sure plastic is not under nori. Hold plate and mold firmly and turn over. Remove mold. Leave sushi wrapped in plastic until ready to serve. Wipe a sharp knife with a damp cloth and cut sushi into bite-sized square, rectangular or diamond shaped pieces. Peel off plastic and serve with soy sauce.

Grilled eggplant and carrot sushi

Makes 8 pieces

²/₃ oz (20 g) ginger, peeled and grated
2 teaspoons Japanese soy sauce
2 tablespoons rice vinegar
2 tablespoons olive oil
1 Japanese eggplant (aubergine)
1 large carrot, peeled and halved lengthwise
3 tablespoons olive oil
2 cups (10 oz/300 g) sushi rice (see page 44)

To make ginger vinaigrette: Whisk together ginger, soy sauce, rice vinegar and olive oil in a bowl. Set aside.

Cut eggplant lengthwise into 6 slices, each ¹/₂ inch (1 cm) thick. Trim off skin from 2 slices to make narrow ribbons.

Using a vegetable peeler, slice carrot lengthwise from cut side to make 5 long, thin, wide slices. Cut 1 slice of carrot into 4 narrow ribbons.

Heat 1 tablespoon olive oil in a grill pan or large frying pan over medium-high heat. Add eggplant slices and cook until golden and tender, 2–3 minutes each side. Transfer to a plate lined with paper towels. Add 1 tablespoon olive oil to pan and repeat with carrot slices.

In a small saucepan, heat remaining 1 tablespoon olive oil over low heat. Add eggplant and carrot ribbons. Cook, stirring gently, for 1 minute. Using a slotted spoon, transfer to paper towels to drain.

Using ¹/₄ cup (1 oz/30 g) sushi rice for each, make 8 oblong-shaped sushi fingers, following the instructions on pages 96–97. Set aside.

Place an eggplant strip on a dry work surface and place a rice ball on one end. Roll up rice ball in eggplant strip, and tie with a carrot ribbon. Repeat with remaining eggplant to make 3 more sushi. Repeat, rolling rice balls in carrot slices and tying with eggplant ribbons, to make 4 more sushi.

Serve with the ginger vinaigrette.

Grilled shiitake sushi

Makes 10 pieces

1 tablespoon Japanese soy sauce
1 tablespoon mirin
10 fresh shiitake mushrooms, stems removed
1 cup (5 oz/150 g) sushi rice (see page 44)
$^1/_2$ nori sheet sliced into 10 strips, $^1/_2$ inch x 3 inches
   (1 cm x 7.5 cm)
finger bowl: water with a splash of rice vinegar

Combine soy sauce and mirin and brush on shiitake. Grill mushrooms until tender, 2–3 minutes. Dip both hands in finger bowl and shake off excess. With one hand, pick up 1 tablespoon of rice and gently squeeze and shape it into a rectangle with rounded edges. Pick up a mushroom with the other hand, bending your fingers to form a shallow mold that mushroom can rest in. Place shaped rice ball on mushroom and very gently press down with index and middle fingers,

holding your thumb at top end of ball to stop rice being pushed out the end.

Turn over rice ball so mushroom is on top and continue gently pushing topping against rice with your index and middle fingers. Turn sushi 180 degrees and repeat. The topping should look like a roof over the rice ball, with very little, if any, rice visible. Place a nori strip on top of the mushroom and tuck each end underneath rice ball to keep the mushroom in place.

Filling variations

- Replace mushrooms with tofu.
- Seasoned omelette slice tied with blanched scallion, or sliced avocado with wasabi mayonnaise and toasted sesame seeds.
- Pickled radish (takuan) and shiso leaf, tied with seasoned kampyo strip.
- Seafood options: sashimi fish (salmon, tuna, kingfish, trevally), squid, cuttlefish and shrimp (prawns).

Jumbo shrimp nigiri-zushi

Makes 10 pieces

10 jumbo shrimp (prawns), washed with heads removed
10 bamboo skewers or long toothpicks
salty boiling water
1 cup (5 oz/150 g) sushi rice (see page 44)

Insert a skewer along shrimp from head to tail, running along legs of shrimp without touching flesh.

Drop shrimp into a pot of salted, boiling water (use enough salt to make it taste like seawater). Boiling shrimp in salted water keeps protein in shrimp. They will sink to bottom, and after 3–5 minutes will change color and rise to top. (Do not use a lid, or a strong smell of shrimp will remain.)

To check that they are cooked, remove one shrimp from water and squeeze gently. If inside is firm, it is cooked.

Quickly place shrimp in ice water to retain color and stop flesh from shrinking and becoming hard. When shrimp are cold, remove from ice water and place in a colander.

Remove skewer, using a screwing motion to avoid breaking flesh. Remove shell from around body, but not tail.

Lay shrimp down with tail away from you, then cut from head to tail along belly with knife only going halfway in.

Use the knife or your fingers to open out and flatten shrimp carefully, without breaking the flesh.

Remove vein and rinse shrimp with mildly salted water. Lay on paper towels to drain.

Either remove tails and cut shrimp in half lengthwise, or leave whole. Make sushi rice and mold as per nigiri-zushi method on pages 96–97. Top each rice ball with a shrimp.

Mango and kimchi nigiri

Makes 8 pieces

1 mango, peeled and cut from pit
2 cups (10 oz/300 g) sushi rice (see page 44)
8 pieces Chinese (napa) cabbage kimchi
1 nori sheet, cut into 8 strips, each $1/2$ inch (1 cm) wide
    and 4 inches (10 cm) long

Cut mango flesh into 8 strips, each about $1^1/4$ inches (3 cm) thick. Shape rice into 8 fingers, following instructions on pages 96–97. Top each rice finger with a mango strip and a piece of kimchi. Tie a nori strip around sushi like a belt, and serve.

Marinated mackerel nigiri zushi

This is a traditional style of sushi. The fish is marinated in a vinegar mixture and then used to make nigiri-zushi. Because it is already seasoned, you may not need as much Japanese soy sauce for dipping. Marinating fish adds to the variety in a mixed sushi plate.

1 mackerel
salt
rice vinegar
Japanese soy sauce, for serving

Use the three-part method to fillet the mackerel (see page 40).

Wet some paper towels, squeeze out excess water and lay damp paper on bottom of a flat-bottomed container.

Sprinkle salt over paper and lay the mackerel fillets skin-side down on salted paper. Sprinkle salt over mackerel. Leave small fish for 2 hours, larger fish for 3 hours.

Remove fillets from container and gently rinse mackerel. Lay on clean, dry paper towel to drain.

Place fillets in a clean, flat-bottomed container. Pour rice vinegar in to cover fish.

Leave small fish for 30 minutes, larger fish for 1 hour. (If you prefer more fish flavor, leave fish in vinegar for a shorter time.)

Drain fillets, wrap in plastic wrap and refrigerate. Use fish the following day for sushi, making sure you have removed all bones.

Omelette sushi

Makes 10 pieces

8 eggs
$^1/_3$ cup (3 fl oz/80 ml) number-one dashi (see page 152)
$^1/_3$ cup (3 oz/90 g) sugar
1 teaspoon mirin
pinch salt
2 tablespoons light Japanese soy sauce
vegetable oil, for cooking
$1^1/_2$ cups (8 oz/250 g) sushi rice (see page 44)
10 nori belts (see below)

1 In a bowl, beat eggs until just blended. Stir in dashi, sugar, mirin, salt and soy sauce. Heat 1–2 tablespoons oil in a square omelette pan over medium heat. Pour excess oil from pan into a bowl with a piece of greaseproof paper or cloth nearby ready to re-oil pan when needed.

2 Pour a thin layer of omelette mixture into pan. Use chopsticks or a spatula to press out any air bubbles.

3 When omelette is firm, run chopsticks around it to loosen.

Using chopsticks, fold one-third of omelette from far side toward center, then fold this two-thirds over remaining one-third to the side closest to you. Add more mixture, lifting cooked omelette up to let it flow underneath. When firm, fold over as before. Continue adding mixture, cooking until firm and folding.

4 Remove from heat and use a wooden board that fits inside the pan to press down and shape the omelette. Turn omelette onto a board. Allow to cool before using or refrigerating.

Cut omelette into strips 1 inch (2.5 cm) wide and 3 inches (7.5 cm) long. Form sushi into fingers (see pages 96–97), using nori belts (see below) to strap omelette pieces to sushi.

Tips

• Nori belt: Take a small strip of nori about $^1/_2$ x 3 inches (12 mm x 7.5 cm) and use this as a belt, as shown above.

• To make a thin, crepelike omelette to use shredded in chirashi-zushi or finely sliced sushi rolls, follow Steps 1 and 2, then Step 4. Cut into fine shreds.

Seasoned carrot sushi

Makes 10 pieces

1 cup (5 oz/150 g) sushi rice (see page 44)
1 large seasoned carrot (see page 229), thinly sliced
  diagonally
10 scallions (shallots/spring onions), green parts only,
  blanched
1 teaspoon peeled and grated fresh ginger
teriyaki sauce (see page 228), for dipping (optional)
finger bowl: water with a splash of rice vinegar

Shape rice into 10 balls. Pick up a seasoned carrot slice with one hand, bending your fingers to form a shallow mold that carrot can rest in. Place shaped rice rectangle on carrot and very gently press down with index and middle fingers, holding your thumb at top end of rectangle to stop rice being pushed out the end. Turn rice so carrot is on top and continue pushing topping against rice with your index and middle fingers. Turn sushi 180 degrees and repeat. The topping should look like a roof over rice, with very little, if any, rice visible.

Tie a scallion around each sushi and garnish with grated ginger. Serve with teriyaki sauce for dipping.

Shiitake mushroom sushi

Makes 10 sushi

10 fresh shiitake mushrooms, stemmed
1 cup (5 oz/155 g) sushi rice (see page 44)
rock or sea salt, for sprinkling
2 lemons, cut into wedges

Using a sharp knife, score mushroom caps with an asterisk pattern, but avoid cutting through flesh. Grill or broil mushrooms for 1–3 minutes, or until tender and darkened. Sprinkle a little salt on mushroom caps.

Make sushi using nigiri-zushi method (see pages 96–97), placing mushrooms either upside down or right-side up.

Serve with lemon wedges. Squeeze lemon juice on top before eating.

Eggplant sushi

Makes 10 sushi

1–2 Japanese eggplants (aubergines), peeled
vegetable oil, for deep-frying
1 cup (5 oz/155 g) sushi rice (see page 44)
white sesame seeds for garnish
$1/2$ cup (4 fl oz/125 ml) Japanese soy sauce
2 tablespoons sugar
1 cup (8 fl oz/250 ml) mirin

Cut eggplant slices into $1/4$ x $1 1/2$ x 2 $1/2$-inch (6-mm x 4-cm x 6-cm) slices. Brush with oil. Deep-fry eggplant for about 2 minutes, or until soft. Drain and cool.

Make sushi using nigiri-zushi method (see pages 96–97) and garnish each with white sesame seeds.

Combine soy sauce, sugar and mirin in a saucepan. Boil to reduce to 1 cup (8 fl oz/250 ml) or $1/2$ cup (4 fl oz/125 ml), depending on your taste. Serve sushi with a little sweet soy sauce on top.

Snow pea sushi

Makes 10 sushi

10 nori belts (see page 104)
1 cup (5 oz/155 g) sushi rice (see page 44)
20 snow peas (mange-touts), blanched and cooled
umeboshi paste or mayonnaise, for garnish

Make sushi using nigiri-zushi method (see pages 96–97).

Wrap nori belts around sushi. Garnish each with a dab of
umeboshi paste or mayonnaise.

Asparagus sushi

Makes 10 sushi

10 asparagus spears, trimmed, blanched and dipped in ice
  water
10 nori belts (see page 104)
1 cup (5 oz/155 g) sushi rice (see page 44)
mayonnaise and red chili seasoning (ichimi togarashi) for
  garnish

Cut asparagus spears 2–3 inches (5–7.5 cm) long and cut
them into lengthwise slices if they are thick.

Make sushi using nigiri-zushi method (see pages 96–97).
Wrap nori belts around sushi. Garnish each with a dab of
mayonnaise and a pinch of red chili seasoning.

Soy nigiri with melted cheese

Makes 8 pieces

2 cups (10 oz/300 g) prepared sushi rice (see page 44)
1 piece salmon, about $6^1/2$–$7^3/4$ oz (200–240 g), cut into
   8 slices, $^1/4$ inch (6 mm) thick, $1^1/4$ inches (3 cm) wide,
   and $2^1/2$ inches (6 cm) long
8 teaspoons Japanese soy sauce
4 slices cheese, halved
8 kinome (prickly ash) or parsley sprigs

Preheat broiler (grill) to medium heat. Line a small baking sheet with aluminum foil. Meanwhile, take one-eighth of rice and shape it into a finger about $^1/4$ inch (6 mm) thick, $^3/4$ inch (2 cm) wide, and 2 inches (5 cm) long. Mold rice and salmon together following instructions on pages 96–97, making sure they are firmly molded, and place on a plate. Repeat with remaining salmon and rice. Pour soy sauce over sushi.

Transfer sushi to baking sheet and place under broiler (grill) as close as possible to the heating element. Broil (grill), turning once, until browned on each side.

Top each sushi with a half cheese slice. Return to broiler (grill) and broil (grill) until cheese has melted. Arrange a sprig of kinome on top of each piece and serve immediately.

Tip
Cheddar cheese slices are particularly suitable for this recipe.

Spicy barbecued eel in cucumber parcels

Makes 8 pieces

8 kombu (kelp) strips, 3 inches (7.5 cm) long and 1 inch
  (2.5 cm) wide
1 teaspoon sugar
2 tablespoons rice vinegar

2 small English (hothouse) cucumbers, halved lengthwise
3 cups (15 oz/450 g) prepared sushi rice (see page 44)
3 oz (90 g) barbecued eel, heated and cut into 8 crosswise
  slices
8 kinome (prickly ash) or sansho pepper (Japanese
  mountain pepper) sprigs
sweet and sour chili sauce, for serving

Cut kombu into 8 ribbons, each ⅛ inch (3 mm) wide and
3 inches (7.5 cm) long. Cook kombu strips in boiling water for
1 minute. Combine the sugar and rice vinegar in a bowl. Add
kombu strips and let sit for 10 minutes.

Using a vegetable peeler, slice cut side of cucumber
lengthwise to make 16 long, thin, wide slices.
  Wet your hands and take one-eighth of sushi rice and form it
into a ball. Insert a piece of eel in center and form into a ball
again. On a dry work surface, place 2 strips of cucumber to
make a cross, and place ball on center. Lift the 4 cucumber
ends to encase the rice, leaving an opening at the top. Tie a
kombu ribbon around the outside to secure. Insert a kinome
sprig in the top. Repeat with remaining ingredients.
  Serve with sweet and sour chili sauce.

Tip
Barbecued eel is available barbecued and frozen. If using
frozen eel, defrost, then heat until warm: about 30 seconds in a
microwave or 2 minutes in an oven.

Tofu sushi

Makes 10 sushi

8 oz (125 g) firm tofu, drained
1 cup (5 oz/155 g) sushi rice (see page 44)
10 nori belts (see page 104)
grated fresh ginger, minced scallions (shallots/spring
  onions), white or red miso paste, or mayonnaise, for
  garnish

Cut tofu into ¼ x 2 x 2½-inch (6-mm x 5-cm x 6-cm) pieces.
  Make sushi using nigiri-zushi method (see pages 96–97).
Wrap nori belts around sushi. Add garnish of your choice.

Avocado sushi

Makes 10 sushi

1–2 avocados, peeled, pitted and sliced
10 nori belts (see page 104)
1 cup (5 oz/155 g) sushi rice (see page 44)
white or red miso paste, for garnish

Use 2 slices of avocado for each sushi piece. Make sushi
using nigiri-zushi method (see pages 96–97). Wrap nori belts
around sushi. Top each with a dab of miso paste.

Hand-wrapped sushi rolls
(Temaki-zushi)

Temaki-zushi are the easiest type of sushi to make at home. They are do-it-yourself hand-rolled cones of nori filled with sushi rice and a variety of other ingredients. You can also use other wrap ingredients, such as omelettes or rice paper rolls. See the following pages for ingredient combinations and suggestions, and step-by-step instructions on how to assemble sushi rolls. They make excellent party food. Simply prepare the fillings ahead of time and lay them out attractively in separate bowls or on one large platter on the table. Give your guests a little guidance on how to make the rolls and then let them make their own, encouraging them to experiment with combinations of fillings. You may also wish to provide each of your guests with a hand towel. Japanese restaurants provide clean, damp hand towels for diners to wipe their hands on. (You can heat them in the microwave and roll them up like cigars for a truly authentic experience.)

Step-by-step
hand-wrapped sushi roll

5 cups (25 oz/780 g) sushi rice (see page 44)
20 nori sheets, halved
wasabi paste

Fillings of choice
salmon or tuna, minced or cut into $1/2$ x $1/2$ x 3-inch (1 x
  1 x 7.5-cm) sticks
jumbo shrimp (king prawns), cooked, shelled, veins and
  tails removed (see page 101)
unagi eel fillets, cut into $1/2$ x $1/2$ x 3-inch (1 x 1 x 7.5-cm)
  sticks
sea urchin or salmon roe
cooked or smoked fish, cut into $1/2$ x $1/2$ x 3-inch (1 x 1 x
  7.5-cm) sticks
omelette, cut into 3-inch (7.5-cm) strips
cucumbers, cut into 3-inch (7.5-cm) lengths, then finely
  sliced lengthwise
avocado slices
sliced or torn lettuce leaves
blanched vegetables such as asparagus, snow peas
  (mange-tout), sliced onion and carrot
white sesame seeds
scallions (shallots/spring onions) or chives, finely sliced

Side dishes
gari (pickled ginger slices)
Japanese soy sauce
wasabi paste
mayonnaise (or mix a little wasabi and lemon juice with
  mayonnaise to make wasabi mayonnaise)

1 Pick up a sheet of nori and hold it flat in your left hand,
rough side up. Take a spoonful of rice and place an oblong
ball of rice on left side of nori. Flatten out rice and make a
groove for other ingredients. With a small spoon, wipe a
little wasabi along rice.

2 Add filling or fillings of choice. Here we are adding long
slices of cucumber and eel.

3 Fold near corner of nori sheet over filling to make a pointed
end.

4 Use fingers to roll nori into a cone shape. Grasp nori to
seal roll.

Serve with individual bowls of gari (pickled ginger slices), soy
sauce, wasabi, mayonnaise and rice.

Aonori crepes rolls

Makes 4 cones

$^3/_4$ cup (4 oz/125 g) canned tuna, drained
2 tablespoons Japanese mayonnaise
2 eggs
1 teaspoon sugar
pinch of salt
1 teaspoon mirin
1 tablespoon aonori (nori) flakes
1 tablespoon canola oil
1 cup (5 oz/150 g) prepared sushi rice (see page 44)
wasabi paste, to taste
1 English (hothouse) cucumber, cut lengthwise into $^1/_4$-inch (6-mm) thick strips
4 nori strips, each 6 inches x $^3/_4$ inch (15 cm x 2 cm)
8 gari (pickled ginger slices), drained
Japanese soy sauce, for serving

In a bowl, combine drained tuna and Japanese mayonnaise and mix well. Set aside.

To make crepes, whisk eggs, sugar, salt, and mirin together in a bowl. Add aonori flakes and stir lightly.

In a nonstick frying pan, heat oil over medium heat. Pour one-quarter of egg mixture into pan, swirling to coat the base. Cook until surface of crepe becomes dry. Turn crepe over and cook for 30 seconds. Transfer to a plate and cover. Repeat with remaining mixture to make 4 crepes.

Place 1 crepe on a dry work surface. With a wet hand, pick up about 1 tablespoon sushi rice and spread over center of crepe, in a triangular shape. Smear with wasabi. Spread tuna mixture over rice and place 2–3 cucumber strips on top. Fold edge of crepe over rice and roll up tightly into a cone shape (see pages 114–115). Wrap a nori strip in a band around end. To seal nori, apply a little water along edge.

Serve with gari and soy sauce.

Broccoli and bell pepper cones

Makes 4 pieces

3 oz (100 g) broccoli, blanched in salted water for 1 minute
  and drained
1/2 red bell pepper (capsicum), seeded
1 1/2 oz (45 g) cold Brie or Camembert cheese
1 cup (5 oz/150 g) sushi rice (see page 44)
2 sheets nori, halved
1 teaspoon wasabi paste
2 tablespoons Japanese mayonnaise

Rinse broccoli under running water until chilled. Drain and pat with paper towels. Cut bell pepper lengthwise into pieces 1/4 inch (6 mm) thick. Slice cheese thinly. Holding a nori sheet half in your left hand, spread one-fourth of rice over almost half of nori and smear wasabi in center. Layer rice with cheese slices, broccoli, and bell pepper. Roll tightly into a cone roll, following instructions on pages 114–115. Repeat with remaining ingredients. Top each piece with 1/2 tablespoon Japanese mayonnaise.

Green tea soba and pistachio

Makes 8 pieces

3½ oz (100 g) green tea soba noodles (available in
Japanese and Asian markets)
2 sheets nori, quartered
1 teaspoon green Tabasco sauce
4 tablespoons (³/₄ oz/20 g) smooth peanut butter
2 tablespoons pistachio nuts, crushed

Soy vinaigrette
1 teaspoon mirin
2 tablespoons rice vinegar
1 tablespoon Japanese soy sauce

In a large pot of salted, boiling water, cook soba noodles until
just tender, following instructions on package. Drain noodles in
a strainer and rinse under running water, occasionally turning
the noodles with your hand, until cold. Drain well.

With dry hands, place 1 nori piece on a dry work surface.
Place one-eighth of soba noodles on nori and sprinkle with
green Tabasco sauce.

Roll following the instructions on pages 114–115, then form
into a wedge shape. Gently but firmly press the end to seal.
Spread with ½ tablespoon peanut butter. Sprinkle with
pistachio nuts. Repeat with remaining ingredients. Arrange
2 pieces on each plate.

To make soy vinaigrette: Combine mirin, rice vinegar and soy
sauce in a bowl and stir. Serve vinaigrette in individual bowls.

Eat with fingers or chopsticks.

Omelette sushi cones

Makes 6 cones

3 thin seasoned omelettes (see page 231)
1 cup (5o z/150 g) sushi rice (see page 44)
1 teaspoon wasabi paste
1–2 fillings (see list below)
2–3 teaspoons beni-shoga
¼ cup (2 fl oz/60 ml) Japanese soy sauce

Suggested fillings
pickled radish (takuan) and seasoned kampyo
  (see page 229)
seasoned carrot (see page 229) and blanched
  snow peas (mange-tout)
pickled radish (takuan) and fresh shiso leaves
cucumber and toasted sesame seeds
sashimi tuna or salmon and shiso leaves; crabmeat and
  cucumber

Cut each omelette in half. Place about 1½ tablespoons sushi rice in middle. Top with a dab of wasabi and 1–2 fillings. Fold omelette over fillings to form omelette into cone shape as per instructions on page 114–115. Serve with beni-shoga and soy sauce.

Prosciutto and baby spinach cone rolls

Makes 4 cones

2 cups (10 oz/300 g) sushi rice (see page 44)
2 nori sheets, halved
1 teaspoon wasabi paste
8 baby spinach leaves
4 prosciutto slices
4 teaspoons Japanese mayonnaise
4 capers
Japanese soy sauce, for serving

Following the instructions on pages 114–115, spread sushi rice on rough side of one piece of nori. Smear wasabi in a line down center of rice. Place 2 baby spinach leaves and 1 slice proscuitto on top. Roll up to form a cone. Top cone with 1 teaspoon Japanese mayonnaise and a caper. Repeat with remaining ingredients. Serve with soy sauce.

Ruby grapefruit and apple mint cone rolls

Makes 4 cones

1 ruby grapefruit (pink grapefruit)
2 cups (10 oz/300 g) sushi rice (see page 44)
4 sprigs apple mint or other mint
2 sheets nori, halved

Honey chili
1 red chili, seeded and thinly sliced
4 teaspoons honey

To prepare grapefruit, cut off ends of grapefruit down to the flesh. Place on one end on a cutting board. Using a small, sharp knife, cut off peel vertically down to the flesh. Holding grapefruit over a bowl, cut on either side of membrane to release segments into the bowl.

Using one-fourth of the grapefruit segments, and spreading sushi rice on rough side of nori, make a cone roll following instructions on pages 114–115. Wrap cone in a 4 x 8-inch (10 x 20-cm) rectangle of cellophane to keep fresh. Insert a mint sprig in the top. Repeat with remaining ingredients to make 3 more rolls.

To make honey chili: Stir together chili and honey in a small bowl. Drizzle over sushi, and serve.

Tempura sushi roll

Makes 8–12 cones

3 cups (24 fl oz/750 ml) vegetable oil for deep frying

1 egg yolk

1/2 cup (3 fl oz/90 ml) iced water

1/2 cup (2 oz/60 g) sifted all-purpose (plain) flour plus extra
   flour for dusting

1 carrot, cut into thin strips 2 inches (5 cm) long

3 oz (90 g) green beans, ends trimmed and halved

red, green or yellow bell pepper (capsicum), cut into thin
   strips 2 inches (5 cm) long

2–3 cups (10–15 oz/300–450 g) sushi rice (see page 44)

1/2 cup (4 fl oz/125 ml) number-one dashi (see page 152)

2 tablespoons light Japanese soy sauce

1 tablespoon mirin

1/4 cup (2 oz/60 g) grated fresh daikon (optional)

1 teaspoon peeled and grated fresh ginger

4–6 sheets nori, halved

8 shiso or small lettuce leaves, shredded or cucumber
   strips (optional)

Pour oil in a large saucepan or deep-fryer and heat until moderately hot (325°F/170°C). While oil is heating, place egg yolk in a bowl and add iced water, mixing lightly, without beating or creating air bubbles. Add measured flour all at once and mix until just combined but still lumpy. Lightly dust vegetables in additional flour, shaking off excess, then dip in batter. Deep-fry vegetables until golden, 2–3 minutes.

Meanwhile, heat dashi, soy sauce and mirin over low heat. Pour into individual dipping bowls. Gently squeeze excess liquid from daikon and place in middle of sauce, topped with ginger.

When vegetables are ready, make sushi cones with nori sheets immediately, as per instructions on page 114–115 adding sushi rice, a tempura vegetable and a lettuce leaf and roll nori around the fillings. Serve with dipping sauce.

Vegetarian cone rolls with balsamic vinegar

Makes 4 cones

1 carrot, peeled
1 daikon, peeled
2 cups (10 oz/300 g) sushi rice (see page 44)
$^1\!/_2$ teaspoon wasabi paste
8 small beet (beetroot) leaves
12 kaiware (radish sprouts) or mustard cress sprouts
12 enoki mushrooms with stems
balsamic vinegar, for dipping

Using a vegetable peeler, cut 4 long, thin, wide strips from carrot, and 4 from daikon. With a wet hand, spread rice on the strips in a triangular shape. Using your index finger, smear wasabi in a line down the center, and place 2 beet leaves, kaiware, and enoki mushrooms over wasabi. Roll up to form a cone as per instructions on page 114–115, gently pushing in the ingredients. Wrap cone in a 4 x 8-inch (10 x 20-cm) rectangle of cellophane to hold it closed. Repeat with remaining ingredients. Serve with balsamic vinegar.

Tip
Kaiware are available in Japanese markets.

Vietnamese rice paper rolls with black rice

Makes 4 rolls

12 small cooked shrimp (prawns), shelled
4 square rice paper sheets
1 cup (5 oz/150 g) black sushi rice (page 44)
1 teaspoon wasabi paste
2 tablespoons peanuts, crushed
4 cilantro (fresh coriander) sprigs, stemmed
8 fresh chives
sweet and sour chili sauce, for serving

Cut shrimp in half from head to tail and remove vein. Soak 1 rice paper sheet at a time in a shallow bowl of warm water for 10 seconds. Drain, pat dry with paper towels, and transfer rice paper to a work surface.

Spread a quarter of rice across center of a rice paper sheet, leaving a 3/4-inch (2-cm) gap at each end of paper.

Dab a little wasabi on rice and sprinkle 1/2 tablespoon crushed peanuts over top. Layer a cilantro sprig and 4 shrimp halves in a line, cut side down, and top with 2 chives. Roll up rice paper to enclose fillings, tucking in one end and leaving other end open, with chives protruding. Repeat with remaining ingredients. Serve rolls immediately with sweet and sour chili sauce.

Tips
- Sweet and sour chili sauce is available from supermarkets and Asian markets.
- Cooked shrimp are available from seafood markets. To cook shrimp, boil in an uncovered saucepan of salted water until they become firm and change color, 3–5 minutes. Remove and place in iced water until cool.

Tofu pouches
(Inari-zushi)

Battleship sushi
(Gunkan maki-zushi)

Inari-zushi have a unique and intriguing flavor, the deep-fried tofu being both savory and sweet. The basic technique for making inari-zushi—deep-fried slices of tofu sliced open and used as pouches for sushi rice and other fillings—can be adapted to make any number of variations. The deep-fried tofu slices, called abura-age-dofu, can be bought from an Asian supermarket, already cooked, or made at home. They are either square or oblong, and can be sliced in a number of ways to form pouches. The type of tofu used to make abura-age-dofu differs from other tofu in that more coagulants have been used. It is sliced thinly, pressed to release moisture, then deep-fried twice. Before you use store-bought pouches, rinse them in boiling water to remove as much oil as possible.

Some ingredients will not stay on top of rice on their own, so with semi-liquid ingredients such as sea urchin and salmon roe, it is necessary to wrap the whole sushi with nori sheets or other wrappers to keep it together. These types of sushi are called gunkan maki-zushi, or battleship sushi. When making gunkan-maki, remember that moist hands are good for touching the sushi rice, but it is best to have dry hands when handling nori. Because nori is like paper, if you are making various kinds of sushi, leave the making of gunkan maki-sushi until last, otherwise the nori will become wet and may break.

Step-by-step
seasoned tofu pouches

Makes 10 pieces

5 pieces 2 x 4-inch (5 x 10-cm) thin deep-fried tofu (abura-age), or 10 pieces 2 x 2-inch (5 x 5-cm)
1 cup (8 fl oz/250 ml) number-one dashi (see page 152) or stock
2 tablespoons superfine (caster) sugar
2 teaspoons sake
2 tablespoons Japanese soy sauce
1$\frac{1}{2}$ cups (8 oz/250 g) sushi rice (see page 44)

Put tofu in a saucepan of boiling water and boil to remove excess oil, about 2 minutes. Drain, gently squeezing out excess water.

In a saucepan, combine tofu, dashi, sugar, sake and soy sauce.

Poke a few holes in a sheet of foil and shape it to fit inside a saucepan so it rests on top of the liquid. This drop-lid allows steam to escape but keeps tofu submerged while cooking. Bring mixture to a boil, reduce heat and simmer for 15 minutes. Remove from heat and cool in liquid.

Drain, squeezing out excess liquid. Gently roll over each piece of tofu with a rolling pin to loosen the center.

Cut each piece in half. Gently ease open cut end of each piece with your fingers, pushing down to each corner to form a pouch. These pouches are now ready to be filled with sushi rice.

1 Cut each piece of rectangular tofu in half to make 2 squares; cut square tofu diagonally to make 2 triangles.

2 Open center of each cut square or triangle to make a pouch. With moist hands, take a ball of sushi rice the size of a golf ball and gently squeeze it together.

3 Fill tofu pouch loosely with sushi rice. (If you fill the pouch too tightly, it will break.)

4 Wrap edges of pouch around rice to form inari-zushi.

Battleship sushi

Makes 8 pieces

1 nori sheet
1 cup (5 oz/155 g) sushi rice (see page 44)
wasabi paste
4 oz (125 g) sea urchin, salmon, ocean trout or tobiko
   (flying fish roe)

Cut the nori into strips about 1 inch (2.5 cm) wide and 6 inches (15 cm) long.

Take a golf ball-sized ball of rice in your hand and gently squeeze it into a rectangular block with rounded edges. Place on a clean board. Repeat with remaining rice.

With one moist hand holding one rice ball, use dry fingers of your other hand to pick up nori sheet.

With rough side of nori facing rice, press end of nori to rice (it will stick) and then wrap nori all around rice. Gently press over-lapping edge of nori to form a complete ring (or use a crushed grain of sticky rice to hold the ends together).

Dab a little wasabi on top of rice, then place roe on top of rice inside ring of nori.

Blueberry sushi with honey chili

Makes 4 pieces

1 English (hothouse) cucumber
1 cup (5 oz/150g) sushi rice (see page 44)
4 tablespoons (1 oz/30 g) blueberries
2 fresh small red chili peppers, halved, seeded, and cut
  into fine julienne

Honey-chili sauce
1 fresh chili, seeded and finely chopped
2 tablespoons honey

Using a vegetable peeler, peel off a wide, lengthwise slice of cucumber skin and discard. Place cucumber on a cutting board, cut side up, hold firmly, and with the peeler, peel a paper-thin slice about 1$\frac{1}{2}$ inches (4 cm) wide and 4 inches (10 cm) long. (The strip will have a narrow green outer edge of skin and white flesh in the center. The skin allows the cucumber to stick to the rice.) Repeat to make 3 more slices.

With wet hands, shape rice into 4 fingers. Wrap a cucumber strip around outside of each rice finger. Top with 1 tablespoon blueberries and 1 chili strip. Place sushi rolls on a plate.

To make honey-chili sauce: Mix chili and honey together in a bowl.

Pour sauce over sushi rolls to serve.

Couscous inari

Makes 4 pouches

1 cup (8 fl oz/250 ml) warm water
1 chicken bouillon cube
1 cup (6 oz/185 g) couscous
4 shiitake mushrooms, stemmed
1 tablespoon Japanese soy sauce
1 tablespoon mirin
2 tablespoons water
4 inari (bean curd pouches), seasoned (see page 128)
4 whole garlic chives for tying, plus 4 garlic chives, finely chopped
4 nori strips, each $^{1}/_{2}$ x 4 inches (1 x 10 cm)
4 teaspoons tobiko (flying fish roe)

In a small saucepan, bring water to a simmer and add bouillon cube. Stir to dissolve cube. Bring to a boil and pour over couscous in a bowl, stirring with a fork. Cover and set aside for 5 minutes. Fluff with a fork.

In a saucepan, combine mushrooms, soy sauce, mirin, and water. Bring to a simmer and cook for 5 minutes.

Open inari from cut side and use a teaspoon to fill with couscous.

Wrap a garlic chive around each inari and secure with a nori strip.

Sprinkle tobikko and chopped chives on top of each inari. Remove mushrooms from liquid, squeeze out excess liquid, then arrange on top of the couscous in each piece.

Grilled chicken ships

Makes 8 pieces

2¹/₄ sheets nori
1 teaspoon canola oil
1 skinless, boneless chicken breast, about 7 oz (220 g)
2 cups (10 oz/300 g) sushi rice (see page 44)
4 tablespoons Japanese mayonnaise
8 small curly endive (curly chicory) leaves
2 tablespoons umeboshi (pickled plum) puree, for serving

Using cooking scissors, cut ¹/₄ sheet of nori into very thin strips. Set aside on a plate.

Also using scissors, cut 2 nori sheets into quarters. Set aside on a dry work surface.

Heat a grill pan over medium-high heat and add oil. Add chicken, reduce heat to medium, and cook until cooked through, about 10 minutes. Transfer chicken to a plate and let cool slightly. With your fingers, shred chicken into fine strips. Transfer to a medium bowl, add mayonnaise and stir well.

With wet hands, mold rice into 8 fingers, following the instructions on pages 96–97.

With dry fingers of one hand, pick up a piece of nori and wrap it around rice (rough side in), sealing on one end and leaving other end open like a pouch. Press shredded chicken onto rice through open nori end. Insert a curly endive leaf and sprinkle with thin nori strips. Repeat with remaining ingredients. Serve with umeboshi puree.

Seasoned tofu roll

Makes 6 rolls (18 pieces)

6 seasoned tofu pouches (see page 128)
1¹/₂ cups (7 oz/225 g) sushi rice (see page 44)
6 strips pickled radish (takuan) ¹/₂ inch (1 cm) thick and
   3¹/₄ inches (8 cm) long
6 strips seasoned kampyo (see page 229)
   about 3¹/₄ inch (8 cm)
1 tablespoon toasted sesame seeds (see page 34)
18 scallions (shallots/spring onions), green parts only,
   blanched then well drained
finger bowl: water with a splash of rice vinegar

Cut open two short sides of seasoned tofu pouches and open out flat, short side toward you, rough side up. Dip both hands in finger bowl, shaking off excess. Spread one-sixth of rice on each tofu sheet, leaving a ¹/₂-inch (1-cm) strip at the front and a ³/₄-inch (2-cm) strip on side farthest away uncovered. Lay 1 strip radish and 1 strip kampyo across center of rice and sprinkle with sesame seeds. Pick up edge of tofu and roll up tightly. Tie 3 scallions around each roll about ³/₄ inch (2 cm) apart. Cut between each tie. Serve some pieces facing up and some on their side for variation.

Tandoori chicken-daikon ships

Makes 8 pieces

1 small boneless, skinless chicken breast,
    about 5$\frac{1}{2}$ oz (170 g)
$\frac{1}{4}$ cup (2 fl oz/60 ml) tandoori paste
1 large daikon, halved and peeled
1 teaspoon canola oil
2 cups (10 oz/300 g) sushi rice (see page 44)
2 tablespoons plain (natural) yogurt
8 caperberries

Vinaigrette
2 teaspoons Japanese soy sauce
1 tablespoon mirin
1 tablespoon rice vinegar

Spread tandoori paste on both sides of chicken and let chicken sit for 20 minutes. Place a daikon half on a cutting board, cut side up, and, holding daikon steady with your hand, use a vegetable peeler to cut 8 long, thin, wide slices. Place slices in a bowl of water and set aside.

Heat a frying pan over medium-high heat and add oil. Add marinated chicken to pan and cook, on both sides, until cooked through. Transfer chicken to a cutting board, let cool slightly, then cut lengthwise into 8 thin slices.

Drain daikon slices and pat dry with paper towels.

With wet hands, mold sushi rice into 8 fingers, following the instructions on pages 96–97. Holding rice with one hand, pick up a daikon slice and wrap it around rice, pressing gently to make sure it sticks to rice. Top with a dollop of yogurt and a chicken slice. Repeat with remaining ingredients. Top each sushi with a caperberry.

To make vinaigrette: Combine all ingredients in a bowl and stir to mix. Divide among individual sauce dishes and serve alongside sushi for dipping.

Vegetarian battleship sushi

Makes 10 pieces

1 teaspoon wasabi paste
2 tablespoons mayonnaise
$1/2$ small avocado, finely diced
1 scallion (shallot/spring onion), green part only, finely
   sliced
1 cup (5 oz/150 g) sushi rice (see page 44)
1 sheet nori, cut into 1-inch x 5-inch (2.5-cm x 13-cm)
   strips
1 teaspoon toasted black sesame seeds
$1/4$ small English (hothouse) cucumber, seeded and finely
   sliced, skin on
$1/4$ cup (2 fl oz/60 ml) Japanese soy sauce
2 teaspoons beni-shoga
finger bowl: water with a splash of rice vinegar

Mix wasabi and mayonnaise until smooth. Carefully fold in avocado and scallion. Dip both hands in finger bowl, shaking off excess. Gently shape about 1 tablespoon of rice into a small oval or rectangle. Place 1 nori strip against rice, shiny side out. Press gently and continue to wrap strip around rice ball. Use a grain of rice to seal overlapped ends of nori.

Cover top of rice with avocado mixture. Sprinkle with sesame seeds. Tuck 3–4 cucumber slices in at one end. Repeat for remaining sushi. Serve with soy sauce and beni-shoga.

Sushi in a bowl
(Chirashi-zushi)

Chirashi-zushi is a great one-dish sushi meal that is easy to prepare at home. Chirashi means "scattered," and this is what you do: fill a bowl with sushi rice and then scatter the ingredients decoratively over the rice. Alternatively, the ingredients can be mixed with the sushi rice. Almost any fish or vegetable can be used—it is up to the cook's imagination as to what it contains. Chirashi-zushi is usually served in beautiful lacquered bowls, but it is also very attractive when served in food itself; for example, eggplants (aubergines), turnips, lettuce cups and tomatoes.

The following recipes use mostly cooked ingredients, but chirashi-zushi is often made with sashimi. Chirashi-zushi often contains ingredients that are not used in other forms of sushi, such as kamaboko (fish cakes), baby corn, bamboo shoots, lotus root and soboro. Other ingredients that go well in chirashi-zushi are crab, avocado, carrot, green beans, bell peppers (capsicums), scallions (shallots/spring onions), unagi eel, squid, thick omelette slices, tofu, sardines and sesame seeds.

If you wish, you can season the sushi rice used for chirashi-zushi with chopped vegetables, green peas, chopped fresh ginger, gari (pickled ginger slices), soboro, crumbled nori, toasted sesame seeds, tofu or strips of deep-fried tofu, or various sauces.

Step-by-step
Sushi in a bowl

Clockwise from back left: carrot and cucumber decoration, shredded thin omelette, shredded nori seaweed, soboro

Clockwise from back left: kampyo, jumbo shrimp and snow peas (mange-tout), ginger, shiitake mushrooms

Suggested ingredients for chirashi-zushi

- Toasted sesame seeds
- Deep-fried tofu (sliced and rinsed in boiling water to remove excess oil, then boiled in $^1\!/_2$ cup (4 fl oz/125 ml) number-one dashi (see page 152) and $^1\!/_2$ cup (4 fl oz/ 125 ml) water until soft)
- Tofu cakes
- Cucumber
- Avocado
- Cooked baby shrimp

Opposite page, clockwise from top left:
1 Kampyo and ginger
2 Shiitake mushrooms and soboro
3 Jumbo shrimp and snowpeas (mange-touts), carrot and cucumber decoration
4 Shredded nori seaweed and shredded thin omelette

Ground beef and eggplant chirashi-zushi

Makes 4 pieces

¼ onion, finely chopped

2 tablespoons rice vinegar

1 teaspoon olive oil

1 teaspoon sugar

1 tablespoon Japanese soy sauce

4 purple baby eggplants (aubergines), about 2 inches (5 cm) in diameter

canola oil for deep-frying

3 oz (90 g) ground (minced) lean beef, stir-fried until color has changed

2 cups (10 oz/300 g) sushi rice (see page 44)

1 teaspoon grated fresh ginger

1 teaspoon wasabi paste

4 quail eggs

4 teaspoons mustard cress

To make onion vinaigrette: Whisk together onion, rice vinegar, olive oil, sugar and soy sauce in a bowl until well combined. Set aside.

Place an eggplant on its side on a cutting board. Using a sharp knife, cut off a lengthwise slice of eggplant about ½ inch (1 cm) thick. Using a teaspoon, scoop out inside of eggplant, leaving stem intact and making a shell about ½ inch (1 cm) thick. Reserve eggplant flesh for another use.

Fill a tempura pan, or deep-fryer one-third full with canola oil and heat over medium-high heat to 365°F (185°C). Deep-fry each eggplant shell separately, occasionally stirring with chopsticks, until soft. Drain eggplant shells, upside down, on wire rack in tempura pan, or in a wire-mesh skimmer, for 30 seconds. Transfer to paper towels.

In a medium bowl, combine meat, sushi rice, ginger, and wasabi paste. Stir to blend, then spoon into each eggplant.

Carefully separate quail eggs, making sure not to break the yolk. Gently slip 1 yolk on top of each eggplant and garnish with mustard cress. Arrange each eggplant on a plate and pour onion vinaigrette around it.

Habanero chili sushi

Makes 4 servings

1 white onion, thinly sliced in round slices
8 tablespoons Japanese mayonnaise
leaves from 8 parsley sprigs, finely chopped
4 thin prosciutto slices cut into fine shreds
1/4 small habanero chili, seeded and finely chopped
1 tablespoon orange juice
2 cups (10 oz/300 g) sushi rice (see page 44)
4 small cooked shrimp (prawns), shelled and deveined
Japanese soy sauce, for serving

Soak onion slices in a bowl of cold water for 10 minutes. Drain well. In a small bowl, combine Japanese mayonnaise, parsley, prosciutto, and chili, and stir to mix. Stir in orange juice and then onion slices.

Divide sushi rice equally among 4 bowls. Spoon one-fourth of chili mixture into each bowl. Top with a shrimp.

Serve with soy sauce.

Tips

- The habanero is said to be the hottest of all chilies. Yellowish-orange in color, it is about the size of a ping-pong ball, but irregular in shape. If possible, wear rubber gloves when handling hot chilies, since they can linger on the skin even after repeated washing.
- Cooked shrimp are available from seafood markets. To cook shrimp, boil in an uncovered saucepan of salted water until they become firm and change color, 3–5 minutes. Remove and place in iced water until cool.

Kampyo and shiitake mushroom chirashi-zushi

Serves 4

1 cucumber
2 cups (10 oz/315 g) sushi rice (see page 44)
³/₄ oz (20 g) seasoned kampyo strips (see page 229)
4 seasoned shiitake mushrooms, stemmed (see page 229),
  cut into ¹/₄-inch (6-mm) strips
2 tablespoons shredded fresh ginger or gari (pickled
  ginger slices)
2 tablespoons soboro
2 tablespoons shredded nori
¹/₂ cup (2 oz/60 g) shredded thin omelette (see page 231)
4 jumbo shrimp (king prawns), cooked, shelled, veins and
  tails removed (see page 101)
5–10 snow peas (mange-tout), blanched
¹/₂ unagi eel, grilled and cut into bite-sized pieces
carrot and cucumber decorations (see page 46)

Cut cucumber crosswise into 2-inch (5-cm) pieces, then into thin, lengthwise slices.

In a large bowl or 4 individual bowls, spread out sushi rice to make a flat bed, keeping it loosely packed. Add following ingredients one by one, sprinkling them to cover the rice and then each other in layers: shredded ginger, kampyo, shiitake mushrooms, soboro, shredded nori and shredded omelette.

Make a decorative display on top with cucumber slices, shrimp, snow peas, eel and decorations.

Do not add soy sauce.

Mango chutney and turnip chirashi-zushi

Makes 8 pieces

8 baby turnips
2 cups (10 oz/300 g) sushi rice (see page 44)
4 teaspoons vindaloo paste
8 teaspoons mango chutney
8 fresh raspberries
8 mango spears, each $^1/_2$ inch (1 cm) wide, and 1 inch (2.5 cm) long

Trim tops of turnips, leaving $^1/_2$ inch (1 cm) of stem intact, and set aside.

Using a small, sharp knife, cut a slice from bottom of each turnip so that they sit upright, then pare the sides to form a hexagonal shape.

Using a teaspoon, scoop out the inside of each turnip, leaving a thin shell. Or cut an $^1/_8$-inch (3-mm) thick slice from top of each turnip and reserve.

In a pot of salted boiling water, cook turnips and reserved tops until tender, about 10 minutes. Transfer to iced water and let cool. Drain upside down on paper towels and pat dry.

Fill each turnip with mango chutney and sushi rice. Spread $^1/_2$ teaspoon vindaloo paste over rice and top with a raspberry. Insert 1 mango slice into rice. Arrange sushi on a plate with a turnip top leaning against the side of each. Eat with fingers.

Tips
- If fresh mango is unavailable, use canned mango.
- Vindaloo paste is an Indian curry paste, similar to madras curry. Purchase in jars or cans from supermarkets and store in the refrigerator after opening.

Parmesan cheese chirashi-zushi in tomato

Makes 4 pieces

1/2 **English (hothouse) cucumber**
4 **vine-ripened tomatoes**
2 **cups (10 oz/300 g) sushi rice (see page 44)**
8 **Parmesan cheese shavings, plus** 1/4 **cup (1 oz/30 g)**
   grated Parmesan
2 **egg yolks**

Olive oil vinaigrette
2 **tablespoons rice vinegar**
1 **tablespoon sugar**
pinch of salt
2 **teaspoons olive oil**
leaves from 4 parsley sprigs, finely chopped

Cut cucumber into lengthwise slices, then cut the slices crosswise in half, 1/16 inch (2 mm) thick. Set aside.

Cut off the top of each tomato and reserve for garnish. With a teaspoon, scoop out the insides, leaving a shell. Blanch tomato shells in salted boiling water for 5 seconds. Using a slotted spoon, transfer tomatoes to ice water. Using your fingers, slip off tomato skins. Transfer to paper towels to drain.

Fill each tomato with one-fourth of sushi rice. Insert 2 cucumber slices and 2 Parmesan shavings on one side of rice. Whisk egg yolks in a bowl and dip outside of stuffed tomato into egg yolk to coat. Place grated Parmesan on a plate and roll the outside of each tomato in it to coat. Arrange tomatoes on individual plates and garnish with tomato lids.

To make olive oil vinaigrette: Whisk together rice vinegar, sugar, salt, olive oil and parsley in a bowl until well combined. Pour 1 teaspoon vinaigrette around each tomato.

Saffron rice and lettuce chirashi-zushi

Makes 4 pieces

Saffron sushi rice
1 teaspoon saffron
1 cup (7 oz/220 g) raw sushi rice
1 cup (8 fl oz/250 ml) water
¼ cup (2 fl oz/60 ml) rice vinegar
2 tablespoons sugar
pinch of salt

Strawberry vinaigrette
¼ cup (2½ oz/75 g) strawberry jam
¼ cup (2 fl oz/60 ml) rice vinegar

1½ oz (40 g) preserved herring roe, chopped
4 fresh chives, finely chopped
4 iceberg lettuce leaves
strawberry leaves for garnish

To make saffron sushi rice: Follow the instructions on page 44, adding saffron to cooling water and mixing cooked rice with vinegar, sugar, and salt. Let cool to room temperature.

To make strawberry vinaigrette: Mix together strawberry jam and rice vinegar in a small bowl.

Add herring roe, and chives to the vinaigrette. Stir to blend together.

Place a lettuce leaf on each of 4 serving plates. Into each leaf, spoon one-fourth of sushi rice to one side. Then spoon one-fourth of herring roe mixture alongside sushi rice. Insert a strawberry leaf as garnish.

Tip
Preserved herring roe is available from Japanese markets. Tobiko (flying fish roe) may be substituted.

Tofu sushi bowl

Makes 4 servings

Marinade
1/4 teaspoon Asian sesame oil
$^3/_4$-inch (2-cm) piece fresh ginger, peeled and grated
1 clove garlic, ground (minced)
1 teaspoon brown sugar
2 tablespoons Japanese soy sauce
$^1/_2$ cup (4 fl oz/125 ml) sake
pinch salt

10 oz (300 g) firm tofu, drained and sliced into pieces
    $^1/_2$ inch (1 cm) thick
6 cups (30 oz/900 g) sushi rice (see page 44)
2 teaspoons toasted white sesame seeds
2–3 tablespoons gari
2 scallions (shallots/spring onions), green parts only, sliced
$^1/_2$ nori sheet, cut into small squares
1–2 teaspoons wasabi paste

To make marinade: Combine sesame oil, ginger, garlic, sugar, soy sauce, sake and salt, stirring until sugar dissolves. Pour marinade over tofu and refrigerate for 20 minutes. Drain well.

In a bowl, combine rice and sesame seeds. Place one quarter of rice in each of 4 deep (donburi-style) bowls. Arrange tofu slices in rosette pattern on top. Lay a few slices of gari across a chopping board, each one slightly overlapping the next. Roll from one end and stand up, folding top out slightly to form a rosebud. Place in center of tofu slices and sprinkle top with scallions and nori squares. Serve with wasabi.

Tips
• Use this marinade for blanched green beans, snow peas (mange-tout), spinach, carrots and sweet peppers and add to Tofu donburi (above) or use in various sushi.
• Seafood option: Substitute sliced sashimi tuna or salmon for tofu.

Vegetarian chirashi-zushi

Makes 4 serves

2 large dried shiitake mushrooms
$1/2$ cup (4 fl oz/120 ml) number-one dashi (see page 152)
2 teaspoons sugar
2 teaspoons mirin
1 small carrot, peeled and julienned
$1/2$ cup ($1^1/2$ oz/45 g) thinly sliced, canned bamboo shoots
2 teaspoons reduced-salt soy sauce
6 thin asparagus spears, blanched
12 snow peas (mange-tout), blanched
1 English (hothouse) cucumber
1 thin seasoned omelette (see page 231)
5 cups (24 oz/750 g) sushi rice (see page 44)
2 tablespoons shredded nori strips
$1/4$ cup shredded beni-shoga
2 teaspoons wasabi paste
$1/3$ cup (3 fl oz/90 ml) Japanese soy sauce

Soak mushrooms in cold water until soft, 20–30 minutes.

Discard stems and slice caps thinly. Put dashi, sugar and mirin in a medium saucepan and bring to a boil over moderate heat. Add carrot strips and simmer until cooked but still crisp, about 2 minutes. Using a slotted spoon, remove from liquid and set aside. Add bamboo shoots, mushrooms and soy sauce to liquid and cook about 5 minutes. Remove from heat. Return carrot strips and allow to cool completely. (This preparation can be done ahead.)

Slice asparagus and snow peas diagonally into $1^1/2$-inch (4-cm) lengths. Cut cucumber lengthwise into quarters and remove seeds. Thinly slice lengthwise into 2-inch (5-cm) pieces or cut decoratively (see garnishes page 46). Roll omelette and slice thinly, separating slices with fingertips.

Place rice in lacquered boxes, individual bowls or on one large platter. Arrange a selection of vegetables decoratively on rice and garnish with omelette, nori strips and beni-shoga. Serve with wasabi and soy sauce.

Sushi soups

There are two basic soups served with Japanese meals. One is the well-known miso, the other is a clear soup called suimono. To make both, you begin with a stock called dashi. Dashi is also the basic ingredient in many other Japanese soups, sauces and traditional dishes and can be used as a substitute for Western-style stocks and consommés. It has a delicate, mildly fishy flavor.

There are two forms of dashi. Number-one dashi is stronger and is used as the base for clear soup. Number-two dashi uses the leftover ingredients from number-one dashi, combined with water, to make a more diluted stock. This is then mixed with miso paste to make miso soup.

These basic soup ingredients are just the start. With them you can add almost any type of food to make delicious soups that are bound to please everyone. The miso paste you use and other ingredients you add will determine the strength of the soup's flavor. Lighter-colored miso pastes generally have a subtle, slightly sweet flavor, whereas the darker, or "red," miso pastes have a saltier, stronger flavor. Experiment with different miso pastes in differing amounts until you find the style that suits you best.

Step-by-step

Basic soup stock

Traditional dashi is made with bonito fish that has been smoked, dried and fermented for several months. The hard bonito is shaved into flakes on a wooden block and simmered in water with a piece of kombu, or dried kelp. People generally use already prepared bonito flakes these days. We recommend making your own dashi using the traditional methods and ingredients because of the quality of the final stock, but as bonito flakes are not cheap and making dashi takes time, instant dashi (hon dashi) may be substituted.

Number-one dashi

Makes 4^1/$_2$ cups (36 fl oz/1.1 L)

4^1/$_2$ cups (36 fl oz/1.1 L) water
1 kombu, 4-inch (10-cm) square
^{1}/$_2$ oz (15 g) bonito flakes

Use a clean, damp cloth to wipe off white film on surface of kombu. In a saucepan, combine water and kombu. Let soak for up to 2 hours, then place over high heat and bring to a simmer. When stock begins to bubble slightly, after about 5 minutes, check center of kombu. If it is soft, remove kombu from saucepan and set aside. If it is hard, continue cooking for a few more minutes, then remove. Let mixture come to boil, then stir. Skim off any bubbles or scum on surface.

Remove from heat and add a small amount of cold water to lower temperature before adding bonito flakes. (Boiling water makes them smell.) Add bonito flakes to saucepan. Do not stir. Use chopsticks to press the flakes down gently to bottom of saucepan. Let rest for 3 minutes.

Lay a cheesecloth or a clean napkin over a colander and strain mixture into a large bowl to remove bonito flakes. Remove the drained bonito flakes and reserve.

If, after tasting the finished dashi, you wish to strengthen its flavor, return mixture to saucepan and simmer for another 5 minutes.

Number-two dashi

Makes 4^1/$_2$ cups (36 fl oz/1.1 L)

reserved bonito flakes and kombu from number-one dashi
4^1/$_2$ cups (36 fl oz/1.1 L) cold water

Put all ingredients into a saucepan. Bring to a boil over high heat and cook for 15 minutes. Remove from heat. Lay a piece of cheesecloth or a clean napkin over a colander and strain mixture into a large bowl. Remove drained bonito flakes. Dashi should be clear.

Tips
- Although some delicate flavour and aromas are lost in storage, you can refrigerate leftover dashi in a sealed container for up to 3 days or freeze for up to 1 month. Freeze in measured amounts such as cup measurements or tablespoons in an ice cube tray.
- Add cooked rice to leftover dashi for a quick and easy soup.

Seaweed stock

Makes 4^1/$_2$ cups (36 fl oz/1.1 L)

about ^{3}/$_4$ oz (20 g) dried kombu (seaweed), 10 inches x 10 inches (25 cm x 25 cm)
4^1/$_2$ cups (36 fl oz/1.1 L) cold water

Gently wipe kombu with a damp cloth. (Never wash kombu as the flavor on the surface will be washed away). Make two or three incisions along edge of kombu to release flavor during cooking.

Put in a saucepan with water and slowly bring to a simmer but do not boil, about 20 minutes. For a stronger flavor, allow longer simmering time. Alternatively, cover kombu with cold water and let stand for 3–4 hours for flavors to be released. Remove kombu and use stock to make clear or miso soup.

Tip
Add dried shiitake mushrooms to stock for added flavor.

Chicken and vegetable hot pot

Makes 4 servings

1 lb (500 g) chicken breast fillets, skin removed and cut
    into bite-sized pieces
6 Chinese napa cabbage leaves, coarsely sliced
$^1/_2$ bunch (6 oz/180 g) spinach
$^1/_2$ carrot, finely sliced
4 scallions (shallots/spring onions), cut into 3-inch (7.5-cm)
    lengths
$^1/_3$ daikon, finely sliced
9 oz (280 g) silken tofu, cut into $^3/_4$-inch (2-cm) cubes
6 oz (180 g) shirataki noodles, cooked in boiling water for
    5 minutes, then drained
4 cups (32 fl oz/1 L) boiling water
1 teaspoon instant dashi
nihaizu sauce (see below), for dipping
2 oz (60 g) grated daikon mixed with $^1/_2$ red chili pepper,
    ground (minced)
2 scallions (shallots/spring onions), thinly sliced
nihaizu dipping sauce (see page 227)

Arrange chicken, vegetables, tofu and noodles attractively on a large platter. This plate is placed on the table and ingredients are cooked in a large pot on a portable burner or in an electric frying pan.

Fill pot or frying pan two-thirds full with boiling water and add instant dashi. Bring stock to a boil. When stock is boiling, add firm vegetables and chicken, then gradually add softer vegetables, noodles and tofu. Diners help themselves, retrieving ingredients and stock with chopsticks or serving spoons when cooked to their liking. Keep adding more raw ingredients to stock as more cooked items are removed. Give each diner a small bowl of nihaizu to which daikon-chili mixture and sliced scallions are added to taste. Diners dip vegetables and seafood into sauce bowl.

Tip
Shirataki noodles are thin, translucent gelatinous noodles made from the starch of a yamlike tuber known as devil's tongue (konnyaku). They can be found both in dry and soft forms in Asian markets and some supermarkets.

Clear soup, popular in Japan, is a simple and subtle soup based on dashi. Many ingredients, such as seafood and vegetables, can be used. The ingredients are not cooked in the soup but are placed in the bowls before the soup is added, so the soup stock remains clear. The delicate flavor goes well with sushi, but also complements other types of Japanese food.

Osuimono (clear soup)

Makes 4 servings

4 cups (36 fl oz/1 L) water
1 small dried shiitake mushroom
$1/2$ teaspoon salt
$1/2$ teaspoon mirin
$1/2$ teaspoon instant dashi, or to taste
4 medium-sized cooked shrimp (prawns), deveined, shells removed and tails intact
4 thinly sliced pieces of white-fleshed fish, approximately $1^1/2$ inches x $^3/4$ inch (4 cm x 2 cm), and $^1/4$ inch (6 mm) thick, boiled
2 oz (60 g) tofu, cut into $^1/2$-inch (1-cm) cubes
1 oz (30 g) enoki mushrooms
1 scallion (shallot/spring onion), thinly sliced
12 mitsuba leaves, for garnish

In a saucepan, bring water, shiitake mushroom, salt and mirin to a boil. Add dashi, stir until well dissolved and remove from heat; add more dashi for a stronger flavor, less dashi for a milder flavor. Remove shiitake mushroom from soup and thinly slice then return to soup.

Place a shrimp in each bowl. Divide fish pieces, tofu cubes, enoki mushrooms, scallions and mitsuba leaves among bowls. Pour soup into each bowl and serve.

Bean-ginger clear soup

Makes 4 servings

4 cups (32 fl oz/1 L) number-one dashi (see page 152)
generous pinch salt
1–2 teaspoons Japanese soy sauce, to taste
$1/3$ cup (2 oz/60 g) green beans, cut into $^3/4$-inch (2-cm) lengths, blanched
4–8 wheaten gluten bread (fu)
1 teaspoon very fine slivers fresh ginger, for garnish

Prepare soup following instructions for Carrot-tofu clear soup (opposite), replacing carrot and tofu with beans and fu, garnished with ginger.

Carrot-tofu clear soup

Makes 4 servings

1 piece carrot 4 inches (10 cm) long, peeled
12 green chives, cut into 4-inch (10-cm) lengths
$1^1/2$ oz (45 g) firm tofu, drained and diced small
4 cups (32 fl oz/1 L) number-one dashi (see page 152)
generous pinch salt
1–2 teaspoons Japanese soy sauce, to taste
1 teaspoon sake
1 teaspoon finely chopped lemon peel, lemon curls or triangle lemon twist (see page 46), for garnish

Make small v-shaped cuts at $^1/2$-inch (12-mm) intervals around carrot. Then cut carrot into $^1/2$-inch (12-mm) slices to make eight flowers. Alternatively, use a biscuit cutter to make flowers. Simmer carrot flowers in boiling water or microwave in a covered container with 1 tablespoon water until cooked but still crisp, 1–2 minutes. Drain. Loosely tie 4 chives into knots. Place one knot, two carrot flowers and one-quarter of the tofu into each of the four soup bowls.

In a medium saucepan, bring stock just to a boil. Stir in salt, soy sauce and sake. Carefully ladle into soup bowls. Garnish with finely chopped lemon peel.

Clear soup with noodles

Makes 4 servings

1 cup (3 oz/90 g) dried, thin somen noodles
4 cups (32 fl oz/1 L) number-one dashi (see page 152)
generous pinch salt
1–2 teaspoons Japanese soy sauce, to taste
8 medium fresh shiitake mushrooms, halved
2 scallions (shallots/spring onions), thinly sliced, for garnish

Bring 4 cups (32 fl oz/1 L) water to a boil in a large saucepan. Add noodles and cook until tender, about 3 minutes. Drain and rinse under cold water.

Prepare soup following instructions for Carrot-tofu clear soup (above), replacing carrot and tofu with noodles mushrooms, and scallions.

Grilled scallops and caviar in miso soup

Makes 4 servings

12 white sea scallops without roe
1 tablespoon mirin
1 tablespoon olive oil
2 cups (16 fl oz/500 ml) water
1$\frac{1}{2}$ tablespoons white miso paste
4 teaspoons salmon caviar
4 scallions (shallots/spring onions), green parts only,
  halved lengthwise, for garnish

Place scallops on a plate and drizzle mirin over them. Heat olive oil in a grill pan or frying pan over medium-high heat. Add scallops to pan, reduce heat to low, and cook on each side until opaque. Transfer scallops to a plate and set aside.

In a medium saucepan, bring water to a boil. Reduce heat to a simmer. In a cup, mix miso paste with 1 tablespoon of the boiling water, and then pour back into saucepan. Add scallops and cook until heated through. Do not overcook. Place 3 scallops in each of 4 bowls and gently ladle soup over them. Top scallops with caviar. Tie each scallion leaf in a knot and place alongside the scallops.

Kobucha soup with fu

Makes 4 servings

1 small leek, including green parts, cut lengthwise into
   4-inch (10-cm) long pieces
8 mushroom-shaped fu (decorative wheat gluten)
2 cups (16 fl oz/500 ml) water
4 teaspoons kobucha (powdered kelp tea)
4 arugula (rocket/mizuna) leaves, for garnish

Slice leeks thinly and soak slices in a bowl of water for
20 minutes. In another bowl of water, soak fu for
10–15 minutes. Drain excess water from fu by hand.

In a small saucepan, bring water to a boil. Add kobucha
powder and stir until dissolved. Remove from heat. Put
2 pieces of fu and some leek slices in each bowl. Fill each bowl
with kobucha mixture. Garnish with an arugula leaf.

Tip
Kobucha, made from kelp and salt, is usually drunk as a tea.
It is available from Japanese markets. If unavailable, a kelp-
seasoning powder may be substituted.

Miso soups

There are many different miso pastes available: some with smooth textures, some chunky, and with varying degrees of flavor and saltiness. Most miso pastes are interchangeable in recipes but quantities may need to be adjusted according to taste. As a general rule, the darker the miso the saltier the taste, and the lighter the miso the sweeter the taste.

Miso soup can be made with a combination of different miso pastes, so experiment with types and quantities. It is advisable to taste miso soup before adding all the miso paste so the taste and saltiness will suit you.

Basic miso soup

Makes 4 cups (1 qt/1 L) miso soup

4 cups (1 qt/1 L) number-two dashi (see page 152)
2 tablespoons (2 oz/60 g) miso paste

Bring dashi to a boil in a saucepan over medium heat.

Put miso paste into a strainer. Hold or place strainer over boiling dashi.

With back of a wooden spoon that fits well into strainer, rub miso so that you sieve it through strainer into boiling stock. Discard any grainy remainders in strainer.

Stir soup as it simmers gently. Check for taste. Remove from heat and serve.

Tips
- Traditionally, miso soup is made with number-two dashi. For a more flavorful miso, you can use number-one dashi (see page 152). If using number-one dashi, you may need less miso paste.
- Miso should be made to taste. Adding more bonito flakes or instant dashi granules to the stock will create a stronger flavor.
- Add almost any vegetable, meat or seafood to the soup, but be sparing with strongly flavored ingredients. The following are ideal: diced scallions (shallots/spring onions), diced tofu, wakame seaweed, daikon radish, corn, scallops, clams, fish, finely sliced shiitake mushrooms, enoki mushrooms, okra, pork, bamboo shoots and asparagus.
- If ingredients need cooking, cook them separately and then add to finished soup. Ingredients such as tofu, enoki mushrooms, scallions (shallots/spring onions) and seaweed do not need cooking; just place them in the serving bowls, pour the hot soup over and serve.

Miso soup with wakame and tofu

Makes 4 servings

¼ cup (⅙ oz/5 g) dried wakame seaweed
4 cups (32 fl oz/1 L) number-two dashi (see page 152
3½ oz (100 g) firm tofu, drained and diced
3 tablespoons red miso paste
2 chopped scallions (shallots/spring onions), green parts only, for garnish

Cover wakame with cold water and let stand to reconstitute and soften, 10–15 minutes. In a large saucepan, bring stock almost to a boil. In a small bowl, dissolve miso with some hot stock, stirring until smooth. Gradually add miso mixture into hot stock. Add tofu and wakame and heat through. Remove from heat and pour into soup bowls. Garnish with scallions and serve.

Tips
- Add enoki, shiitake, shimeji mushrooms or a combination of all three.
- Add bamboo shoots and wakame seaweed.
- Try cooked potato and wakame seaweed, beans or spinach.
- Daikon and deep-fried tofu (abura-age) also make a delicious variation of this soup.

Daikon-carrot miso soup

Makes 4 servings

⅓ cup (2 oz/60 g) daikon (white radish), peeled and julienned
1 small carrot, peeled and julienned
4 cups (32 fl oz/1 L) number-two dashi (see page 152)
3–4 tablespoons white miso paste, to taste
2 scallions (shallots/spring onions), thinly sliced, for garnish
shichimi togarashi (7 spice mix), optional, for garnish

In a large saucepan, bring daikon, carrot and stock to a boil. Reduce heat and simmer until vegetables are cooked but still crisp, 3–4 minutes. In a small bowl, dissolve miso with some hot stock, stirring until smooth. Gradually add miso mixture into hot stock. Bring almost to a boil, remove from heat and pour into soup bowls. Garnish with scallions and schichimi togarashi.

Variation
Schichimi togarashi is a spice mix based on hot peppers. It can be replaced with thinly sliced lemon peel or grated fresh ginger.

Salmon rice soup

Makes 4 servings

4 oz (125 g) salmon fillet, thickly sliced
½ teaspoon salt
4 cups (32 fl oz/1 L) water
1½ teaspoons instant dashi
4 cups (8 oz/760 g) cooked short-grain rice, heated
¼ teaspoon matcha
2 tablespoons wakame seaweed, soaked in warm water
    for 2 minutes
2 scallions (shallots/spring onions), thinly sliced, for
    garnish
wasabi paste, for serving

Preheat broiler (grill). Place salmon slices in a single layer in a baking dish and sprinkle with salt. Broil (grill) salmon for about 2 minutes. Turn carefully with a spatula and cook on second side until almost cooked through, about 1 minute. Remove from heat.

Meanwhile, place water in a saucepan and bring to a boil. Add dashi and stir until well dissolved. Remove from heat. Divide rice among 4 bowls, sprinkle with matcha powder and top with wakame and slices of grilled salmon. Pour soup into each bowl and garnish with scallions. Serve with wasabi.

Tip
Spinach leaves added to the water as it is brought to a boil make a delicious addition.

Seafood hot pot

Makes 4 servings

12 oz (375 g) white-fleshed fish fillets such as snapper or
    flathead
8 mussels, scrubbed and debearded
8 clams, well scrubbed
12 jumbo shrimp (green king prawns), heads and shells
    removed, tails intact, deveined
$\frac{1}{2}$ carrot, thinly sliced
5 oz (150 g) daikon, thinly sliced
6 Chinese napa cabbage leaves, thickly sliced
8 fresh shiitake mushrooms
$\frac{1}{2}$ bunch (6 oz/180 g) spinach
2 stems shungiku
4 scallions (shallots/spring onions), cut into 3-inch
    (7.5-cm) lengths
10 oz (300 g) silken tofu
4 cups (32 fl oz/1 L) boiling water
1 teaspoon instant dashi

2 oz (60 g) harusame (cellophane noodles), soaked in hot
    water for 5 minutes then drained
8 tablespoons grated daikon, mixed with $\frac{1}{2}$ red chili
    pepper, ground (minced)
2 scallions (shallots/spring onions), thinly sliced
nihaizu sauce, for dipping (see page 227)

Arrange fish, shellfish, vegetables and tofu attractively on a
large platter. This platter is placed on the table, and the
ingredients are cooked at the table in a large pot on a portable
burner or in an electric frying pan.

    Fill pot or frying pan two-thirds full with boiling water and add
instant dashi. Bring stock to a boil. When stock is boiling, add
firm vegetables, then gradually add seafood, fish, other
vegetables, tofu and harasume in batches. Diners help
themselves, retrieving vegetables, seafood and tofu from stock
pot with chopsticks when cooked to their liking. Keep adding
raw ingredients to stock as cooked ingredients are removed
and eaten. Give each diner a small bowl of nihaizu to which
daikon-chili mixture and scallions are added to taste.

Tempura soba

Makes 2 servings

5 oz (150 g) dried soba or udon noodles

2 cups (16 fl oz/500 ml) water

¼ cup (2 fl oz/60 ml) Japanese soy sauce

¼ cup (2 fl oz/60 ml) mirin

1 teaspoon instant dashi

4 jumbo shrimp (green king prawns), shells removed, tails left intact, deveined

4 green beans, tops and tails removed

2 slices of bell pepper (capsicum)

tempura batter (see pages 76 for shrimp tempura instructions and page 122 for vegetable tempura instructions)

2 pinches very fine strips of nori, for garnish

Bring a saucepan of water to a boil. Add soba or udon noodles and stir to keep them from sticking together until water returns to boil. Reduce heat slightly and gently boil noodles until cooked, about 5 minutes for soba noodles, about 10 minutes for udon (taste noodles to check if cooked). Drain and rinse in cold water to stop cooking process.

Place water, soy sauce, mirin and dashi in a saucepan and bring to a boil. Remove stock from heat. Follow instructions for tempura shrimp (see page 76) and tempura vegetables (see page 122) to cook shrimp and vegetables, draining them well on paper towels. Reheat noodles by dipping quickly in boiling water for 1 minute. Place noodles in 2 bowls and pour hot stock over noodles. Arrange tempura vegetables and shrimp on top of noodles. Garnish with nori strips.

Tofu hot pot

Makes 4 servings

1 teaspoon instant dashi
1 stem shungiku, cut into 4-inch (10-cm) lengths
2 leaves Chinese napa cabbage, sliced
3 fresh shiitake mushrooms
1 lb (500 g) tofu, cut into 2½-inch (6-cm) cubes
nihaizu diping sauce (see page 227) or Japanese soy
    sauce
3 tablespoons finely grated daikon mixed with ¼ small red
    chili pepper, ground (minced)
scallions (shallots/spring onions), finely sliced

This dish is usually cooked and served in the same pot or in small cast-iron pots or heat-proof casseroles. A dipping sauce is served separately.

Fill a large pot three-quarters full with water. Add instant dashi and bring to a boil. Add shungiku, cabbage and mushrooms and cook until softened, 4–5 minutes. Add tofu and heat through.

Serve with a small bowl of nihaizu or soy sauce for dipping. Keep the daikon mixture and scallions separate, to be added to dipping sauce to taste.

Tip
Shungiku refers to chrysanthemum leaves and they are used as a vegetable. They have a strong flavor, not unlike that of spinach.

Decorative sushi

Just as you can experiment with different fillings in sushi, you can also use fillings to create strikingly decorative sushi rolls. You may like to use food coloring to dye the rice. The way you lay the ingredients out on the flat nori sheets and rice will affect the final design of your roll. Try putting all the ingredients together in the center. Laying ingredients flat along the rice gives a whirlpool effect to the final roll.

Due to the worldwide popularity of sushi, its image has changed. While it maintains its unique Japanese tradition, the ways of preparing sushi in Japan and elsewhere have evolved to include new and modern creations that utilize an incredibly wide variety of ingredients. Only rice has remained the essential ingredient.

Once you acquire the basic skills for making traditional sushi, you can then modify the taste to produce sushi that you feel comfortable with and excited about offering to family and friends. There is no limit to what can be created.

Avocado and papaya wedges

Makes 4 servings

1 ripe but firm avocado
5 oz (150 g) papaya (paw paw)
4 oz (125 g) shredded daikon
8 shiso leaves
sushi rice (see page 44) to serve
10 lemon slices, halved

Wasabi mixture
1 tablespoon wasabi paste
2 tablespoons light Japanese soy sauce
1 tablespoon mirin

Slice avocado in half, remove pit, and peel. Cut each half in half lengthwise. Slice avocado into rectangles.

Cut papaya in half and remove seeds. Cut each half in half lengthwise, using the same style as avocado.

Divide shredded daikon among 4 plates, and place 2 shiso leaves on each plate. Sandwich lemon slices between avocado and papaya slices and 1 section of avocado slices on shiso leaves. In a bowl, combine all ingredients for wasabi mixture.

Serve as a side dish with other sushi and sushi rice.

Black rice rolls with apricot glacé

Makes 12 pieces

Apricot glacé
12 dried apricots
$1/2$ cup (4 fl oz/125 ml) water
$1/4$ cup (2 oz/60 g) sugar
1 teaspoon Grand Marnier liqueur
1 teaspoon sake (Japanese rice wine)

1 sheet nori, halved
1 cup (5 oz/150 g) black sushi rice (page 44)
$1/2$ teaspoon chili paste

To make apricot glacé: Combine apricots and water in a saucepan and bring to a boil over high heat. Reduce heat to low, add sugar, and cook for 10 minutes. Add Grand Marnier and sake and cook, stirring occasionally, until most of the liquid has been absorbed. Remove from heat and set aside to cool.

Cover a sushi mat with plastic wrap. Place a nori half sheet on plastic, shiny side down, and, with wet fingers, spread half the black sushi rice all over nori. Holding surface of rice with one hand, turn over rice and nori, placing rice on the plastic. Using your index finger, smear half chili paste over nori and arrange 6 cooked apricots in center.

Using a sushi mat, roll following instructions on pages 50–51, enclosing fillings and leaving one-fourth of nori uncovered at end farthest from you. Lift up mat and roll forward to join nori edges. Press gently to firm shape.

Unroll mat, remove plastic, and transfer roll to a cutting board. Wipe a sharp knife with a damp towel and cut roll in half; then cut each piece into 3, wiping knife after each cut. Repeat with remaining ingredients. Arrange sushi on plates and serve.

Camellia sushi

Makes 10–12 pieces

1 thin seasoned omelette (see page 231), cut in 2-inch
   (5-cm) squares
4 shiso leaves or 4 pieces nori, cut into 1¹/₂-inch
   (4-cm) squares
2 teaspoons wasabi paste
2 cups (10 oz/300 g) sushi rice (see page 44)
2 teaspoons finely chopped pickled radish (takuan)
2 teaspoons finely chopped gari or beni-shoga
1 scallion (shallot/spring onion), green part only, finely
   sliced
¹/₄ cup (2 fl oz/60 ml) Japanese soy sauce
pesticide-free camellia or lemon leaves cut into edible
   flower shapes, for serving
finger bowl: water with a splash of rice vinegar

Dip both hands into finger bowl, shaking off excess. Place a slice of omelette and shiso leaf in center of a cloth or plastic wrap. Spread a dab of wasabi in middle. Gently shape about 2 tablespoons of rice into a small ball and set on top of wasabi. Gently twist cloth or plastic with your finger and, through cloth, make a small indent in center of each ball. Unwrap carefully and place on a plate. Fill indent with finely chopped radish, gari or scallion. Repeat for remaining balls. On a platter, arrange camellia or lemon leaves around sushi and serve with soy sauce.

Variations
Seafood options: Thin slices smoked or sashimi salmon or tuna with salmon roe or flying fish roe or finely chopped egg yolk in the center.

Dragon rolls

Makes 4 pieces

1 sheet nori, halved
2 cups (10 oz/300 g) sushi rice (see page 44)
$1/2$ English (hothouse) cucumber, halved lengthwise,
  seeded, then cut into strips $1/4$ inch (6 mm) thick
$1/2$ fillet barbecued eel, cut into strips
1 avocado, halved, pitted and peeled
4 teaspoons umeboshi (pickled plum) puree
Japanese soy sauce, for serving

Cover a sushi mat with plastic wrap. Place a half sheet of nori on plastic, shiny side down, and, with wet fingers, spread half sushi rice evenly over nori. Holding surface of rice with one hand, turn over rice and nori so rice is on plastic and nori is on top. Arrange cucumber and eel strips in center of nori. Using sushi mat, roll to enclose fillings, leaving a $3/4$-inch (2-cm) strip of nori visible at end farthest from you. Lift up sushi mat and roll following instructions on pages 50–51.

Press gently to firm shape and seal nori.

Unroll mat, remove plastic, and transfer roll to a cutting board. Wipe a sharp knife with a damp towel and cut roll in half. Repeat with remaining ingredients.

With a small sharp knife, slice an avocado half thinly, keeping slices together, and place it over a sushi roll, pushing gently with your fingers to curve avocado slices. Repeat with other avocado half. Arrange rolls on serving plates and top each piece with 3 drops umeboshi puree. Serve with soy sauce. Eat with a knife and fork.

Tips

• Barbecued eel is sold in airtight bags from Japanese and other Asian markets, and some fish stores.
• Umeboshi (pickled plum) puree is sold in tubes and bottles in Japanese markets.

Heart sushi with aonori paste and gold leaf

Makes 4 pieces

2 cups (10 oz/300 g) sushi rice (see page 44)
1 teaspoon wasabi paste
1 hard-boiled egg yolk, sieved (egg mimosa, see page 77)
1 snapper fillet, about 5$\frac{1}{2}$ oz (170 g), cut into 4 pieces
8 teaspoons aonori paste
1 sheet edible gold leaf

Immerse a small heart-shaped mold, such as a cookie cutter, in a bowl of water. Transfer it to a work surface. Using a wet teaspoon or chopsticks, put sushi rice in mold, leaving a quarter of the mold empty. Holding mold with one hand and pushing top of rice with other hand, carefully remove mold from the formed rice. (Alternatively, use plastic wrap as for triangle rolls, page 184). Repeat with remaining rice.

Smear a small amount of wasabi thinly over rice and top with one-quarter of egg mimosa and a piece of fish. Spread 2 teaspoons of aonori paste over fish and top with a piece of gold leaf. Repeat with remaining ingredients.

Place heart sushi on serving plates and serve. Eat with chopsticks or a knife and fork.

Tip
Edible gold leaf is available from stores that sell cake decorations. It is also added to sake (Japanese rice wine) on special occasions.

Leaf sushi

Makes 2 rolls (12 pieces)

1–2 English (hothouse) or telegraph cucumber, skin on
1^{1}/$_{2}$ sheets nori
1 cup (5 0z/150 g) sushi rice (see page 44)
1 teaspoon wasabi paste
1 tablespoon gari
^{1}/$_{4}$ cup (2 fl oz/60 ml) Japanese soy sauce
finger bowl: water with a splash of rice vinegar

Trim cucumber to the same length as nori sheet, 7^{1}/$_{4}$ inches (18 cm). (Two cucumbers may be needed if using small cucumbers.) Cut cucumber lengthwise into quarters and remove seeds and half the flesh. Cut large nori sheet in half lengthwise, parallel with lines marked on rough side. Cut one half nori sheet lengthwise into strips the same width as cucumber. Join two pieces of cucumber together with a strip of nori in middle. Place one half nori sheet lengthwise on a bamboo mat, about 3 slats from edge closest to you, shiny side down. Cover with rice, leaving a ^{1}/$_{2}$-inch (1 cm) strip on both long sides uncovered. Spread a dab of wasabi and the cucumber across rice ^{1}/$_{2}$ inch (1 cm) from edge of rice farthest away, making sure cucumber extends fully from end to end.

Using your index finger and thumb, pick up bamboo mat and, holding cucumber in place with other fingers, roll forward tightly until rice touches rice on opposite side. Tuck nori around and gently shape roll into a tear drop shape. Unroll mat and place roll on cutting board. Wipe a sharp knife with a damp cloth and cut roll into 6 pieces, wiping knife after each cut. Repeat for remaining roll. Serve with gari, soy sauce and remaining wasabi.

Variation

Replace cucumber with strips of pickled radish (takuan) and seasoned kampyo (see page 229) with nori strips between cucumber pieces.

Lobster tempura rolls

Makes 4 pieces

Dipping sauce
$1/2$ cup (4 fl oz/125 ml)
  rice vinegar
1 tablespoon sugar
1 tablespoon mirin
1 tablespoon soy sauce

1 lobster tail
1 nori sheet
1 cup (5 oz/150 g) sushi
  rice (see page 44)
2 tablespoons katakuri
  starch or cornstarch

Tempura
canola oil, for deep-frying
a few drops Asian
  sesame oil
1 cup (5 oz/150 g)
  tempura flour
1 cup (8 fl oz/250 ml) cold
  water
2 chives, finely chopped
1 hard-boiled egg yolk,
  sieved (egg mimosa)

To make dipping sauce: Combine rice vinegar, sugar, mirin and soy sauce in a bowl and mix well; set aside. Beginning on the softer underside of lobster, insert tip of a large knife and cut meat from shell, leaving meat in a whole piece. Transfer meat to a board and slice it in half, making sure not to cut all the way through and leaving $1/2$ inch (1 cm) uncut, then open it to

have 1 large flat slice of lobster. Trim meat to three-quarters of size of nori sheet.

Arrange nori sheet, shiny side down, on a sushi mat. Place lobster meat on nori and, with wet fingers, arrange sushi rice over lobster. Roll following instructions on pages 50–51. If nori is dry, wet edge and press mat to seal. Place katakuri starch on a flat plate and coat lobster roll. Allow roll to rest, seam side down, for 2 minutes. Unroll mat and transfer roll to a cutting board. Wipe a sharp knife with a damp towel and cut roll into 4 even pieces, wiping knife after each cut. Fill a tempura pan, or deep-fryer one-third full with canola oil and heat over medium-high heat to 365°F (185°C). Add a few drops of sesame oil.

Meanwhile, to make tempura batter, put tempura flour in a medium bowl and gradually whisk in cold water until mixture resembles a light pancake batter. Dip 2 rolls in batter and deep-fry, turning as necessary, until golden. Using a wire-mesh skimmer, transfer to a wire rack, or paper towels, to drain. Set aside on paper towels. Repeat with remaining rolls. Transfer rolls to serving plates and top with egg mimosa and chives. Serve with prepared dipping sauce.

Mille-feuille sushi with blue cheese and pastrami

Makes 4 pieces

1 scallion (shallot/spring onion)
6 oz (185 g) pastrami slices
1 teaspoon wasabi paste
4 tablespoons Japanese mayonnaise
2 cups (10 oz/300 g) sushi rice (see page 44)
4 tablespoons (1 oz/30 g) blue cheese
1 tablespoon pine nuts
4 nori strips, each $^{1}/_{2}$ inch (1 cm) wide and 4 inches
   (10 cm) long
8 beet (beetroot) leaves

Cut scallion in half lengthwise, then cut each piece in half again to make 4 strips. Place in a bowl of cold water to let curls form.

Place a small hexagonal mold on each slice of pastrami in turn, then cut around the mold with a small knife to make 8 hexagonal pastrami shapes.

Combine wasabi paste and Japanese mayonnaise in a small bowl. Stir to blend.

Cut a piece of plastic wrap about 6 inches (15 cm) long and place loosely inside mold. Place $^{1}/_{4}$ cup (1 oz/30 g) sushi rice in mold and press down with a wet rice paddle. Spread 1 tablespoon blue cheese over sushi rice and lay a pastrami shape on top. Add another $^{1}/_{4}$ cup (1 oz/30 g) sushi rice and top with another piece of pastrami. Holding plastic wrap, remove sushi from mold and transfer to individual plates. Spread wasabi mixture over pastrami and top with a few pine nuts and a small curl of scallion. Repeat with remaining ingredients.

Wrap a nori strip around the bottom of each sushi. Arrange with 2 beetroot leaves.

New Yorker rolls with spicy sirloin

Makes 8 pieces

canola oil, for deep-frying
1 scallion (shallot/spring
  onion), finely shredded
1 carrot, peeled and finely
  shredded

Thai basil sauce
1 tablespoon rice vinegar
1 teaspoon fish sauce
2 fresh Thai basil leaves,
  finely chopped
1 teaspoon packed brown
  sugar

1 tablespoon canola oil
2 oz (60 g) sirloin, thinly
  sliced
³/4 nori sheet
1 cup (5 oz/150 g) sushi
  rice (see page 44)
2 fresh cilantro (coriander)
  leaves
1 clove garlic, crushed
¹/4 teaspoon wasabi paste

Fill a tempura pan or deep-fryer one-third full with canola oil and heat over medium-high heat to 365°F (185°C). Fry scallion until golden brown. Transfer to paper towels to drain. Repeat with carrot. Set aside.

To make Thai basil sauce: Combine rice vinegar, fish sauce, basil and sugar in a bowl and mix well. Set aside.

Heat 1 tablespoon oil in a frying pan over medium heat, and cook sirloin, turning once, until rare, about 3 seconds. Transfer sirloin to a plate to cool.

Place nori on a bamboo sushi mat, glossy side down, and spread sushi rice over it. Place sirloin slices over three-quarters of nori, toward the front, and with wet hands spread sushi rice over sirloin. With your index finger, smear wasabi and garlic across center. Top with cilantro.

Using your index finger and thumb, pick up edge of sushi mat nearest to you. Place remaining fingers over fillings to hold them as you roll the mat forward tightly. Press gently and continue rolling forward to complete roll. Gently press mat to shape and seal roll. Unroll mat and transfer roll to a cutting board.

With a dampened knife, slice roll in half. Place 2 pieces side by side and cut them in half; then cut each half again, wiping knife after each cut. Top 4 pieces with fried onion and remaining 4 pieces with carrot. Serve with thai basil sauce.

Pink rice rolls with chili jam

Makes 4 pieces

2 cups (14 oz/440 g) raw sushi rice or short-grain rice
2 cups (16 fl oz/500 ml) beet (beetroot) juice in place of
    water
2 tablespoons strawberry jam
1 teaspoon chili paste
2 tablespoons rice vinegar
1 teaspoon chili paste
1 tablespoon Japanese mayonnaise
4 round rice paper sheets
2 scallions (shallots/spring onions), quartered lengthwise

Prepare sushi rice following the instructions on page 44, but substitute beet juice for cooking water. This creates the "pink" color of the rice.

To make chili jam sauce: Mix together strawberry jam, chili paste and rice vinegar in a small bowl, and set aside.

In another small bowl, mix chili paste and Japanese mayonnaise. Set aside.

Divide pink sushi rice into 4 equal portions and shape into 4 balls.

Soak 1 rice paper sheet at a time, for 10 seconds, in a shallow dish of warm water. Drain and pat dry with paper towels. Transfer to a clean work surface. Place a pink sushi rice ball in center of a sheet of rice paper and, using a spoon, spread chili mayonnaise on top. Wrap like a parcel, folding in the top and bottom, then rolling up. Then wrap 1 strip of scallion around each roll and tie with a knot. Serve with chili jam sauce.

Rainbow rolls

Makes 6 pieces

3 arugula (rocket) leaves
3 beet (beetroot) leaves
1 slice cuttlefish or squid
1 slice salmon
1 slice king fish or yellowtail
1 cooked shrimp (prawn), about $2^3/_4$ inches (7 cm) long,
    without head, shelled, halved and deveined
1 slice mango
1 cup (5 oz/150 g) sushi rice (see page 44)
$^1/_2$ teaspoon wasabi paste
Japanese soy sauce, for serving

Cover a sushi mat with plastic wrap. Beginning from one edge of mat, line up arugula and beet leaves one after another, placing them on a slight diagonal, and leaving some space in between for cuttlefish, salmon, king fish, shrimp, and mango slices. Place fish and mango slices in between arugula and beet leaves.

With wet fingers, form sushi rice into a bar and place on top. Using your index finger, smear rice with a dab of wasabi. Lift up sushi mat and firmly roll sushi, following instructions on pages 50–51.

Unroll mat and transfer roll to a cutting board. Wipe a sharp knife with a damp towel, and cut roll in half. Cut each half into 3 pieces, wiping knife after each cut. Remove plastic and serve with soy sauce.

Tips

- In Japan, this sushi is called Tazuna-zushi, which means string-shaped hand rolls. The wrapping reveals the colorful ingredients and makes it more enticing to taste.
- Cooked shrimp are available from seafood markets. To cook shrimp, boil in an uncovered saucepan of salted water until they become firm and change color, 3–5 minutes. Remove and place in iced water until cool.

Sea urchin

Makes 4 servings

¹/₂ nori sheet
1 English (hothouse) cucumber
5¹/₄ oz (155 g) sea urchin roe
8 kinome (Japanese pepper) sprigs or daikon sprouts
wasabi paste, for serving
Japanese soy sauce, for serving
sushi rice (see page 44), for serving

Cut nori sheet in half. Dip cucumber in water. Place cucumber on nori sheet and roll tightly. Trim both sides of cucumber ends so cucumber does not protrude from roll, then cut roll into 8 pieces.

Place 2 slices of sea urchin roe on cut side of cucumber roll, and top each sea urchin with kinome. Place 2 cucumber rolls in each bowl and serve with wasabi, soy sauce and sushi rice.

Square sushi

Makes 8 pieces

4 cups (20 oz/600 g) sushi rice (see page 44)
food coloring
3 sheets nori
1 strip pickled radish (takuan), thick seasoned omelette
(see page 231) or cooked carrot, cut $^5/_8$ inch x 7 inches
(1.5 cm x 18 cm) thick
finger bowl: water with a splash of rice vinegar

Divide rice in half and add 1–2 drops of food coloring to one
half, leaving half the rice white.

Slightly overlap one full nori sheet and two-thirds of a second
nori sheet, sealing sheets with a few grains of rice. Dip both
hands in finger bowl, shaking off excess. Spread white rice
over half the nori and colored rice over the second half, leaving
a $^3/_4$-inch (2-cm) strip on side farthest from you uncovered.
Pick up edge of nori nearest you and roll tightly to the end.
Wipe a sharp knife with a damp cloth and cut roll lengthwise

into quarters, pressing knife forward so roll does not break
apart.

Slightly overlap one full nori sheet with remaining one-third
nori sheet, sealing with a few grains of rice. Place on bamboo
mat. Arrange cut rolls along edge closest to you so they form a
square, cut sides outward, with radish strip in center. Pick up
edge of the mat nearest you, roll forward, shaping gently with
mat to form a square roll. Unroll mat and place roll on cutting
board, seam on bottom. Wipe a sharp knife with a damp cloth
and cut roll into 8 pieces, wiping knife with each cut.

Variation
Use half sheets of nori to make small square rolls.

Square sushi with tuna and edible flowers

Makes 4 pieces

7 oz (200 g) fresh tuna block
2 cups (10 oz/300 g) sushi rice (see page 44)
8 fresh chives
4 edible flowers, such as violas or nasturtiums
$^3/_4$ x 2-inch (2 x 5-cm) piece ginger, peeled and grated
wasabi paste, for serving
Japanese soy sauce, for serving

Trim the tuna block to a $2^1/_2$-inch (6-cm) square that is 3 inches (7 cm) thick.

Boil water and pour into a heatproof, nonmetallic bowl. Immerse tuna block in boiling water for a few seconds to blanch the outer surface. Transfer to clean paper towels and pat dry.

Place tuna block on a cutting board. Using a large, sharp knife, cut tuna block horizontally into 4 squares, each $^3/_4$ inch (2 cm) thick.

Place a piece of plastic wrap on a work surface. Wet a $2^1/_2$-inch (6-cm) square mold and place on plastic wrap. Using a rice paddle, put one-fourth of sushi rice in the mold and press to form. With wet hands, remove the mold and plastic wrap, pushing over the rice with one hand. Place a tuna square on molded rice and top with an edible flower or serve them on the plate. Repeat with remaining ingredients.

Tie 2 chives around each rice square. Serve with grated ginger, wasabi, and soy sauce on the plate. Eat with a knife and fork.

Tip
Packets of edible flowers are sold in some specialty food stores.

Sushi bars

Makes 2 rolls (16 pieces)

1 English (hothouse) cucumber
pickled radish (takuan)
2 green shiso leaves
2 strips seasoned kampyo (see page 229)
$1/3$ red bell pepper (capsicum), seeded
$1/4$ teaspoon salt
3 cups (15 oz/450 g) sushi rice (see page 44)
1 tablespoon toasted white sesame seeds
1–2 teaspoons wasabi paste
1–2 tablespoons gari
$1/4$ cup (2 fl oz/60 ml) Japanese soy sauce
finger bowl: water with a splash of rice vinegar

Cut cucumber in half and thinly slice, lengthwise. Sprinkle with salt and let stand until soft and pliable. Cut cucumber, radish, shiso, kampyo and bell pepper into strips $2^{1}/_{2}$ inches (7 cm) long. Lay a piece plastic wrap on bamboo mat and alternate half of vegetable strips diagonally across middle, until the arrangement is about 8 inches (20 cm) long. Spread a thin layer of wasabi across the middle. Dip both hands into finger bowl, shaking off excess. Shape half rice into rough bar shape and place on vegetables. Pick up mat with fingers and roll over rice, pressing firmly and gently pulling plastic forward so it is clear of roll. Complete roll with vegetables on top. Allow to set 1–2 minutes. Unroll mat but leave roll in plastic wrap. Wipe a sharp knife with a damp cloth and cut into 8 pieces, wiping knife after each cut. Carefully peel off plastic. Repeat for remaining roll. Serve with gari and soy sauce.

Variations
- Substitute other thinly sliced vegetables, including prepared pickled vegetables which are readily available at Asian markets, such as zucchini, char-grilled eggplant, scallions (green part), seasoned tofu and tempeh.
- Seafood options: smoked or sashimi salmon, chives.

Triangle rolls with dried mango and jumbo shrimp

Makes 8 pieces

1 sheet nori
12 slices dried mango
1 cup (5 oz/150 g) sushi rice (see page 44)
1 teaspoon red horseradish sauce
3 cooked jumbo shrimp (prawns), shelled and deveined
Japanese soy sauce, for serving

Place nori sheet on a sushi mat, shiny side down. Place dried mango slices in rows over three-fourths of nori and, with wet fingers, spread sushi rice over mango. Spread red horseradish sauce across center and top with shrimp.

Roll tightly, following the instructions on pages 50–51, but, while rolling, use pressure from your fingers to form roll into a triangular shape.

Unroll mat and transfer roll to a cutting board. Wipe a sharp knife with a damp towel and cut roll in half; then cut each piece into 4, wiping knife after each cut. Arrange pieces on serving plates. Serve with soy sauce.

Tips

- Cooked shrimp are available from seafood markets. To cook shrimp, boil in an uncovered saucepan of salted water until they become firm and change color, 3–5 minutes. Remove and place in iced water until cool.
- Red horseradish sauce is so coloured because it has been preserved in beet juice.

Triangle sushi with tobiko, wasabi and daikon

Makes 4 pieces

1 daikon, peeled
1 cup (5 oz/150 g) sushi rice (see page 44)
4 tablespoons (1 1/4 oz/40 g) wasabi tobiko
1 tablespoon wasabi paste
nandina leaves or small camellia leaves, for garnish
Japanese soy sauce, for serving

Using a vegetable peeler, cut daikon lengthwise into 4 long, thin, wide slices. Place them in a bowl of water and set aside.

Place a triangle mold, with a base 2 inches (5 cm) wide, on a cutting board and place a piece of plastic wrap loosely inside mold. Using a wet rice paddle, put one-fourth of sushi rice in mold and press to shape. Carefully remove mold, invert rice onto a work surface, and, holding rice with one hand, peel off plastic wrap. Repeat with remaining ingredients. Spread 1 tablespoon tobiko evenly over each.

Drain daikon slices and pat dry with paper towels. Using your index finger, spread a small amount of wasabi over center of each daikon slice. Wrap a daikon slice, wasabi side in, around the bottom of a sushi. Repeat with remaining daikon slices. Transfer each sushi onto an individual plate. Insert a nandina leaf in the center of each for garnish, and serve with soy sauce. Eat with a knife and fork.

Tip
Nandina is also known as Japanese sacred bamboo. It is an evergreen, grown for its elegant structure and leaf colour.

Wisteria sushi

Makes 4 rolls (32 pieces)

6 snow peas (mange-tout), trimmed
2 cups (10 oz/300 g) sushi rice (see page 44)
¼ cup (1 oz/30 g) finely diced pickled radish (takuan)
2 sheets nori
1–2 teaspoons wasabi paste, for serving
2 tablespoons gari, for serving
¼ cup (2 fl oz/60 ml) Japanese soy sauce, for serving
finger bowl: water with a splash of rice vinegar

In a saucepan, gently boil snow peas until just cooked but still crisp, 1–2 minutes. Rinse under cold running water to prevent over-cooking and set color. Finely chop. Stir chopped snow peas through half the rice and radish through remaining rice. Cut each nori sheet in half across lines marked on rough side. Lay one half nori sheet lengthwise on bamboo mat, about 3 slats from edge, shiny side down.

Dip both hands in finger bowl, shaking off excess. Spread one-half of one rice in center of nori, leaving a ½-inch (1-cm) strip of nori on long side farthest away uncovered. Pick up edge of mat nearest you and roll forward so rice on one side touches rice on far side. Unroll mat. Gently press edges together to form a teardrop-shaped roll, tucking small nori strip around end. Repeat for remaining rolls.

Place 4 rolls next to each other on a cutting board. Wipe a sharp knife with a damp cloth and cut all rolls in half. Cut each half into 4 pieces, wiping knife between cuts. Turn each row of teardrop sushi pieces up so the rice is displayed on top. Arrange two rows next to each other to resemble a spray of wisteria flowers. Serve with wasabi, gari and soy sauce.

Tips

- These rice rolls are a delicious solution for nori cut the wrong way—across lines marked on rough side of sheet, as opposed to parallel to lines. These will be longer, but not as wide, so you will have less to wrap around rice and fillings. These sheets can be used to make sushi rolls but with less rice and fillings, or to make wisteria rolls.
- Try blanched asparagus or seasoned baby carrots as fillings.
- Finely chop gari or beni-shoga, pickles, vegetables or herbs and fold through rice.

Sashimi

Sashimi means "raw" in Japanese. A wide variety of fish and seafood can be enjoyed as sashimi, allowing you to experience the full, natural flavor and texture of fish in season. Sashimi is sliced and prepared in various ways, depending on the texture of the ingredient being used, and then decoratively presented. Sashimi is usually eaten at the beginning of a meal, as a light appetizer. Various dipping sauces and accompaniments are used to enhance the flavors of the fish.

While its origins are unknown, there is a very old tradition in Japan of always serving sashimi with an odd number of slices.

Blanched snapper sashimi

Makes 4 servings

3¹/₂ oz (105 g) cucumber
21 oz (625 g) whole snapper
8 lemon slices, halved
pesticide-free flowers, for garnish
wasabi paste, for serving
Japanese soy sauce, for serving

Using a vegetable peeler, remove skin from cucumber. Cut into very thin, fine strips using a sharp paring knife. Place in a bowl of cold water until using.

Remove scales from snapper (see Tips). Fillet into 3 pieces (see page 40) and remove any remaining bones with tweezers. Place a snapper fillet on a platter, skin side up. Pour boiling water over fish (see picture above center). When skin shrinks, transfer fish to a plate and refrigerate until cold. Repeat with second fillet. Before serving, slice fish using the following rectangular slicing technique. While holding a fillet in the left hand, place sharp edge of knife perpendicular to the fillet and cut into slices ¹/₂ inch (1 cm) wide. When cutting each slice leave each piece in its original cut position. (See picture above right.) You should have 20 pieces. Place 5 pieces on each plate. Slip lemon slices between pieces. Garnish with cucumber slices and flowers.

Serve with wasabi and soy sauce for dipping.

Tips

- Blanching has two functions: to cook the skin and outer layer of fish and to give fish an attractive appearance. When a fish is blanched, the skin shrinks and resembles the bark of pine trees (matsukawa). This method suits fish with large scales and firm skin, such as snapper, ocean perch and silver bream.
- For blanched snapper sashimi, the texture is best when snapper weighs 2 lb (1 kg) or less. Larger snapper have thicker, tougher skin.
- Silver bream can also be used for blanched sashimi.
- Scaling can be messy, so work on paper, at the sink or in a clear plastic bag. Holding head of fish and using a scaler (see picture top left), move scaler carefully against scales, working from tail to head. Rinse fish occasionally to make scaling easier.

Blanched tuna cubes

Makes 4 servings

10 oz (300g) tuna block, trimmed of dark flesh and skin
12 small shiso leaves or maple leaves, for garnish
pesticide-free flowers, for decoration
Japanese soy sauce, for serving

Cut tuna block into 2 pieces, approximately 1 inch x 8 inches (2.5 cm x 20 cm) or 1 inch x 6 inches (2.5 cm x 15 cm)—size of pieces will depend on size of block. Bring a saucepan of water to a boil and, using tongs or chopsticks, dip each tuna piece in water for 2 seconds. Remove immediately and place in a bowl of iced water. Refrigerate until chilled. Remove tuna from bowl, and cut into 1-inch (2.5-cm) cubes. Lay a maple leaf or basil leaf over each plate. Divide leaves among 4 plates. Top with tuna cubes, cut side up. Garnish with flowers.

Tip
Salmon can be used instead of tuna.

Bonito sashimi

Makes 4 servings

6½ oz (200 g) sashimi-grade bonito fillet
2 cups (5 oz/150 g) shredded daikon, rinsed then soaked
   in iced water until ready to use
½ small red chili pepper, (ground) minced, mixed with 4
   tablespoons finely grated daikon, for garnish
2 teaspoons peeled and finely grated fresh ginger, for
   garnish
1 scallion (shallot/spring onion), thinly sliced, for garnish
pesticide-free flowers, or carrots cut into flower shapes,
   for decoration
½ cup (4 fl oz/125 ml) tosa shoyu (see page 228)

Cut bonito fillet into 1-inch (2.5-cm) thick pieces. Carefully thread each fillet onto a long metal skewer. Light a gas flame and turn each fillet directly over hot gas flame and quickly sear. (If gas flame is not available, prepare a fire in a grill and place fish fillets on a grill rack and quickly sear, or brown on both sides in a ridged grill pan over high heat.) Bonito should be just seared, and raw in the center. Immediately place bonito in iced water to halt the cooking process. Refrigerate for 30 minutes or until ready to use.

Remove bonito strips from skewer and cut into 1-inch (2.5-cm) cubes. Drain shredded daikon and divide among 4 bowls. Place mounds of tuna on daikon, then garnish with daikon-chili mixture, grated ginger and scallions. Decorate with flowers or carrot shapes. Serve with tosa shoyu and the grated daikon, chili, ginger and scallions added from each bowl to the sauce.

Bonito with egg mimosa

Makes 4 servings

4 hard-boiled egg yolks, sieved (egg mimosa, see page 77)
1 whole bonito, about 21 oz (625 g)
1 teaspoon English mustard or Japanese karashi
3¹/₂ oz (105 g) shredded daikon
pesticide-free flowers, for decoration
Japanese soy sauce, for serving

Preheat oven to 320°F (160°C/Gas 2¹/₂). Spread sieved egg evenly over a small baking sheet lined with aluminum foil. Place in preheated oven and cook until golden brown, about 2 minutes. Set aside.

Fillet bonito into 3 pieces (see pages 40), remove any remaining bones with tweezers, and cut into 1-inch (2.5-cm) cubes. Place bonito in a bowl and toss with mustard. Add cooked yolk and toss again. Divide daikon among 4 bowls. Top with bonito and garnish with flowers.

Serve with soy sauce.

Tip
Myoga is a crispy, juicy and aromatic condiment. If myoga (Japanese ginger) is available, chop 3 oz (100 g) finely and add to bonito cubes.

Combination sashimi

Makes 3 servings

3¹/₂ oz (105 g) shredded daikon
4 rectangular tuna slices (pages 42–43)
4 rectangular salmon slices (pages 42–43)
2 cucumber leaves, for garnish
2 cooked jumbo shrimp (king prawns)
3 rolled cuttlefish with okra pieces
   (see page 68)
2 leaf-shaped wasabi

Wasabi leaves
2 teaspoons wasabi powder
1 teaspoon water

soy sauce, for serving

Prepare ingredients just before serving. Place shredded daikon on a plate. Arrange tuna and salmon slices on opposite sides of plate. Put cucumber leaves between salmon and tuna slices. Place shrimp in front of cucumber leaves and rolled cuttlefish in front of shrimp.

To make wasabi leaves: Mix wasabi powder with water to form a smooth paste. On the plate, shape paste into 2 small ovals and, using a butter knife, shape each oval like a leaf.

Serve with soy sauce for dipping.

Tip
You can use kingfish or garfish instead of tuna and salmon.

Garfish sashimi

Makes 4 servings

4 whole garfish
12 small bamboo leaves, for garnish
16 capers
wasabi paste, for serving
Japanese soy sauce, for serving

Fillet each garfish into 3 pieces (see page 41). Remove skin from fillets.

Cut each fillet along the silver center line into 2 pieces. Place 3 bamboo leaves on each plate. Roll each garfish slice and place 4 rolls on each plate. Top each rolled garfish with a caper.

Serve with wasabi and soy sauce.

Hint
If garfish is unavailable, whiting can be used instead.

Julienned cuttlefish sashimi

Makes 4 servings

2 cuttlefish
1 teaspoon sake
2 tablespoons tobiko (flying fish roe)
1 hard-boiled egg yolk, sieved (egg mimosa), for garnish
1 scallion (shallot/spring onion) leaf, about 4 inches
   (10 cm) long, julienned lengthwise, for garnish
Japanese soy sauce, for serving

Clean cuttlefish (see page 69), and julienne fillets by placing on cutting board and using the tip of the knife to cut thin slices. Be careful, as cuttlefish are slippery. Place fillet slices in a bowl and sprinkle with sake. Add tobiko and mix to combine. Divide among 4 bowls and sprinkle with sieved egg yolk. Slice scallion leaf into 4 thin strips and garnish cuttlefish.

Serve with soy sauce for dipping.

Tip
If cuttlefish is unavailable, squid (calamari) can be used instead. Peel off outer skin layer of squid before eating raw.

Lemon sole with chives

Makes 4 servings

3¹/₂ oz (105 g) shredded carrot
8 taro potato leaves or large basil leaves, for serving
  (optional)
21 oz (625 g) whole lemon sole
1 bunch chives
4 daikon flowers (see page 46)
wasabi paste, for serving
Japanese soy sauce, for serving

Divide shredded carrot among 4 plates. If using, place 2 taro potato leaves on each plate, and set aside until ready to use. Fillet lemon sole into 3 pieces (see pages 40). Place fillet skin down on board, and insert knife just below the skin. While supporting fillet with left hand, gently cut parallel to the chopping board to remove skin. Starting from the left of the fillet, cut into diagonal slices, inclining the blade to the right at a 45-degree angle. Once the fish is cut, raise the blade to a 90-degree angle and slide each slice to the left.

Chop chives into 1-inch (2.5-cm) lengths. Lay a lemon sole slice on a board, place 3 lengths of chives in the center and fold lemon sole in half. Place lemon sole on top of taro leaf. Place a daikon flower on each plate. Serve with wasabi and soy sauce for dipping.

Tip
Flounder can be used instead of lemon sole.

Lightly broiled bonito tataki

Makes 4 servings

21 oz (625 g) whole bonito
1/4 cup (2 oz/60 g) salt, for grilling
1 white onion, thinly sliced
2 scallion (shallot/spring onion) leaves, finely chopped
2 oz (60 g) green ginger, grated
1 clove garlic, crushed and chopped
3 1/2 oz (105 g) shredded daikon
4 red radish flowers (see page 46), for garnish

Vinegar mixture
1/2 cup (4 fl oz/125 ml) rice vinegar or white vinegar
1 teaspoon mirin
1 tablespoon sugar

Fillet bonito into 3 pieces (see page 40) and remove any remaining bones with tweezers. Skewer 3 pieces under skin with bamboo or metal skewers. Holding fillets tightly, press salt evenly onto skin. Broil (grill) uncovered skin side of fillet, until scorched lightly. Place gently in a bowl of iced water. Rinse off salt, remove skewers from fillets, place on a plate and refrigerate for 30 minutes. In a bowl, combine all ingredients for vinegar mixture. Add sliced onion, scallion, ginger and garlic. Combine well.

Remove bonito from refrigerator and slice using the following rectangular technique. While holding a fillet in the left hand, place sharp edge of knife perpendicular to the fillet and cut into slices 1/2 inch (1 cm) wide. When cutting each slice leave each piece in its original cut position. Divide daikon among 4 plates. Arrange bonito on plates. Top with onion slices and scallions. Drizzle with vinegar mixture. Garnish with radish flower.

Tip
Bonito in spring has a very light and subtle taste, whereas in autumn it is very oily and has a remarkably deep texture. In winter, it has more fat on the flesh.

Marble beef tataki

Makes 4 servings

Vinegar mixture
¹/₂ cup (4 fl oz/125 ml) rice vinegar or white vinegar
1 teaspoon mirin
1 tablespoon sugar

1 white onion, finely sliced
2 scallion (shallot/spring onion) leaves, finely chopped
10 oz (300 g) beef sirloin (rump) block
green leaves such as bamboo or camelia leaves, for
    decoration
2 oz (60 g) grated red radish
wasabi paste, for serving
Japanese soy sauce, for serving

Combine all ingredients for vinegar mixture in a bowl. Place white onion in mixture. Add scallion leaves. Bring a saucepan of water to a boil. Add beef and blanch for 10 seconds. Remove beef from saucepan and add to vinegar mixture while beef is hot; toss well. Refrigerate for 30 minutes. Remove marinated beef from mixture and slice thinly. Arrange slices in a flower shape on a plate. Place marinated white onion slices and chopped scallion in center. Garnish with leaves.

Serve with wasabi and soy sauce for dipping. Accompany with grated radish in a side plate. Each plate serves 2.

Tip
The beef can be broiled (grilled) rather than blanched.

Marinated garfish with kelp

Makes 4 servings

4 whole garfish

Vinegar mixture
¼ cup (2 fl oz/60 ml) rice vinegar or white vinegar
1 pinch salt
1 teaspoon mirin, for seasoning
1 tablespoon water

4 dried kelp strips, each 1 inch x 8 inches (2.5 cm x 20 cm), rinsed
4 daikon flowers (see page 46), for garnish
4 scallion (shallot/spring onion) leaves, knotted, for garnish
wasabi paste, for serving
Japanese soy sauce, for serving

Fillet garfish into 3 pieces (see page 41). Remove any remaining bones with tweezers. In a bowl, combine all ingredients for vinegar mixture. Soak kelp strips in mixture for 10 minutes. Place garfish fillet on board. Top with kelp strip and another garfish fillet, stacking like a sandwich. Pressing garfish and kelp with your hands, add in the vinegar mixture. Repeat with remaining garfish and kelp. Refrigerate for 30 minutes. Before serving, trim ends of each garfish and kelp sandwich neatly and cut into ³/₄-inch (2-cm) pieces. Divide pieces among 4 plates. Garnish with daikon flowers and scallion leaves.

Serve with wasabi and soy sauce for dipping.

Tips
- When cutting garfish and kelp, wrap the sandwich in a nori sheet to make cutting easier.
- Whiting can be used instead of garfish.

Marinated mackerel sashimi

Makes 4 servings

21 oz (625 g) whole mackerel
1 tablespoon salt

Marinade
1 cup (8 fl oz/250 ml) rice vinegar or white vinegar
2 tablespoons sugar
1 tablespoon mirin

3¹/₂ oz (105 g) shredded daikon
4 lemon wedges, for garnish
Japanese soy sauce, for serving

Fillet mackerel into 3 pieces (see page 40) and remove any remaining bones from each fillet with tweezers. Place fillets on a platter and sprinkle with salt. Refrigerate for 30 minutes. In a bowl, combine marinade ingredients. Remove mackerel from refrigerator and add marinade. Refrigerate for 30 minutes.

Remove mackerel from refrigerator and wipe off excess moisture with a kitchen cloth. Slice using the following rectangular technique. While holding a fillet in the left hand, place sharp edge of knife perpendicular to the fillet and cut into slices ¹/₂ inch (1 cm) wide. When cutting each slice leave each piece in its original cut position. You should have 20 slices.

Divide daikon among 4 plates. Place 4 mackerel slices on each plate. Garnish with a lemon wedge. Serve with soy sauce.

Tip
Yellowtail may be used in place of mackerel.

Ocean perch with plum puree

Makes 4 servings

10 oz (300 g) whole ocean perch
3¹/₂ oz (100 g) umeboshi (pickeled plum puree)
1 shiso leaf, finely chopped
1³/₄ oz (50 g) shredded daikon
1 shiso leaf, julienned, for garnish

Scale fish (see Tip on page 188) and fillet into 3 pieces (see page 40). Remove any remaining bones with tweezers. Broil (grill) fillets lightly on skin side only, over direct fire or on an uncovered broiler (grill), until the skin just changes color. Slice using the following rectangular technique. While holding a fillet in the left hand, place sharp edge of knife perpendicular to the fillet and cut into slices ¹/₂ inch (1 cm) wide. Mix the plum puree and chopped shiso leaves together. Divide shredded daikon among 4 plates. Arrange sliced fish on each plate, and top with puree. Sprinkle with julienned shiso.

Tip
Jewfish or baby snapper can be used instead of ocean perch.

Paper-thin John Dory

Makes 4 servings

21 oz (625 g) whole John Dory
1/2 cup (4 fl oz/125 ml) ponzu (Japanese citrus vinegar) or
    rice vinegar
juice of 1 lemon or 4 pieces dried or frozen yuzu
6 lemon slices, halved, for garnish
16 daikon flowers (see page 46), for garnish
4 carrot flowers (see page 46), for garnish

Scale fish (see Tip on page 188) and cut into 3 pieces (see page 40). Remove any remaining bones with tweezers. Then remove skin. With a sharp knife, trim left side of fillet diagonally. While holding the cut fillet with the left hand, incline the blade at a 45-degree angle to your left. Slice thinly, like paper, from the left to the right of the flesh. Slice each fillet thinly into pieces 2 inches x 1 inch (5 cm x 2.5 cm). Gently place on a plate with chopsticks or a fork. Mix vinegar and lemon juice in a small bowl. Serve vinegar sauce with sashimi. If using yuzu, put one piece into each dipping sauce bowl. Add 3 lemon slices, 4 daikon flowers and a carrot flower to each serve.

Tips

- Plates in a color that contrasts with the fish are recommended, as the color of the plate can be seen through the paper-thin slices. If you have caviar, sprinkle some over the sashimi.
- Snapper can be used instead of John Dory.

Salmon sashimi

Makes 4 servings

3¹/₂ oz (105 g) ugo (salted seaweed) or shredded daikon
10 oz (300 g) salmon fillet without skin, bones removed
4 daikon flowers (see page 46), for garnish
wasabi paste, for serving
Japanese soy sauce, for serving

Rinse ugo under running water for 10 seconds to extract extra salt, then leave in cold water until needed. Slice salmon using the following rectangular technique. While holding a fillet in the left hand, place sharp edge of knife perpendicular to the fillet and cut into slices ¹/₂ inch (1 cm) wide. When cutting each slice leave each piece in its original cut position. Place ugo on each plate and arrange 7 slices on top of ugo. Place daikon flower in middle.

Serve with wasabi and soy sauce.

Salmon tataki

Makes 4 servings

10 oz (300 g) salmon fillet, skin removed
2 chive stems, chopped
40 g ginger, grated
1 teaspoon mirin
1 pinch salt
8 shiso leaves
8 quail eggs
red maple leaves, for decoration (optional)
wasabi paste, for serving
Japanese soy sauce, for serving

Remove any bones in salmon with tweezers. Julienne fillet, then using a knife, chop finely with the chives and ginger. Mix in mirin and salt. Form into 8 small balls.

Cut shiso leaves in half lengthwise along the center vein and wrap each salmon ball with 2 leaf halves. If necessary, use a little water to help leaves adhere. Place 2 wrapped salmon balls on each plate. Break a quail egg in a bowl. Carefully spoon out yolk and place on top of salmon. Decorate plate, if desired, with maple leaves.

Serve with wasabi and soy sauce for dipping.

Tip
Ocean trout can be used instead of salmon.

Salmon with blue cheese and white miso puree

Makes 4 servings

8 oz (250 g) salmon or ocean trout fillet, skin removed
1³⁄₄ oz (50 g) scallions (shallots/spring onions), shredded
1 teaspoon sansho seeds (Japanese mountain pepper)

Puree
1 oz (30 g) blue cheese
1³⁄₄ oz (50 g) white miso paste
2 tablespoons mirin
1 tablespoon light Japanese soy sauce

Place fillet skin down on board, and insert knife just below the skin. While supporting fillet with left hand, gently cut parallel to the chopping board to remove skin. Starting from the left of the fillet, cut into diagonal slices, inclining the blade to the right at a 45-degree angle. Once the fish is cut, raise the blade to a 90-degree angle and slide each slice to the left.

Whisk blue cheese and white miso in a bowl. Add mirin and light soy sauce. Arrange shredded scallion on 4 plates. Place salmon on the scallion on each plate and top with blue cheese sauce and sansho seeds.

Tips
- If you prefer a lighter taste, add 1 tablespoon of sour cream to the sauce.
- Sansho is a bitter-tasting Japanese pepper. Sansho is usually bought ground, since it keeps its aroma well. Usually, sansho seeds are sold after being cooked with soy sauce, sugar, kelp stock and other ingredients.

Snapper with egg mimosa and tobiko

Makes 4 servings

2 hard-boiled egg yolks, sieved (egg mimosa, see page 77)
21 oz (625 g) whole snapper
2 tablespoons tobiko (flying fish roe)
mustard sprouts, for garnish
Japanese soy sauce, for serving

Spread egg evenly over a small baking sheet covered with aluminum foil. Place in the oven and cook egg until golden brown, about 2 minutes. Set aside.

Fillet snapper into 3 pieces (see page 40) and remove any remaining bones with tweezers. Thinly slice each fillet, starting from the left of the fillet, cutting into diagonal slices, and inclining the blade to the right at a 45-degree angle. Once the fish is cut, raise the blade to a 90-degree angle and slide each slice to the left.

Place snapper pieces and tobiko in a bowl and toss together. Add toasted mimosa and toss lightly. Garnish with mustard sprouts.

Tip
Instead of flying fish roe, salted herring roe can be used. It is similar in size to flying fish roe, but light yellow and saltier.

Trumpeter sashimi

Makes 4 servings

20 oz (600 g) whole trumpeter
3¹/₂ oz (105 g) shredded daikon
8 thin lime slices, halved
4 red radish flowers (see page 46), for garnish
1 hard-boiled egg yolk, sieved (egg mimosa)
8 chives, stemmed
wasabi paste, for serving
Japanese soy sauce, for serving

Fillet trumpeter into 3 pieces (see page 40) and remove bones. Place fillet skin down on board, and insert knife just below the skin. While supporting fillet with left hand, gently cut parallel to the chopping board to remove skin. Holding a fillet in the left hand, place sharp edge of knife perpendicular to the fillet and cut into slices ¹/₂ inch (1 cm) wide. While cutting each slice, slide knife from base to tip of blade in one continuous movement, then move remaining whole fillet away from cut slices, using tip of knife. Do not push cut pieces away. You should have 20 slices.

Place a small amount of shredded daikon on each plate and top with 5 trumpeter slices. Slip 4 lime slices between trumpeter slices.

Garnish with a radish flower. Place egg mimosa into each flower. Garnish with 2 chives. Serve with wasabi and soy sauce for dipping.

Tips
- It is best to fillet trumpeter and remove skin just before serving.
- Mullet is a good substitute for trumpeter.

Tuna sashimi

Makes 4 servings

6¹/₂ oz (200 g) sashimi-grade tuna fillet
2 cups (5 oz/150 g) shredded daikon, rinsed then soaked
   in iced water until ready to use
¹/₂ small red chili pepper, (ground) minced, mixed with 4
   tablespoons finely grated daikon
2 teaspoons peeled and finely grated fresh ginger
1 scallion (shallot/spring onion), thinly sliced
pesticide-free flowers, or carrots cut into flower shapes,
   for decoration
¹/₂ cup (4 fl oz/125 ml) tosa shoyu (see page 228)

Cut tuna fillet into 1-inch (2.5-cm) thick pieces. Drain shredded daikon and divide among 4 bowls. Place mounds of tuna on daikon, then garnish with daikon-chili mixture, grated ginger and scallions. Decorate with flowers or carrot shapes. Serve with tosa shoyu, adding the grated daikon, chili, ginger and scallions from each bowl to the sauce.

Tuna with yam puree

Makes 4 servings

10 oz (300 g) tuna, trimmed of dark flesh and skin
2 tablespoons Japanese soy sauce
1³/₄ oz (50 g) shredded daikon
3¹/₂ oz (105 g) yam or kumara puree
1 nori sheet, shredded

Cut the tuna into 1-inch (2.5-cm) cubes (see right). Place in a bowl, add soy sauce, and gently toss. Divide daikon among 4 bowls. Place tuna cubes on daikon in each bowl. Pour the yam puree over tuna and garnish with shredded nori.

Tip
Yam puree is available packaged from Japanese grocery stores.

Cubic sashimi (kaku-zukuri)

Kaku-zukuri is a modern sashimi technique that was developed to create sashimi slices of a uniform size and thickness. This technique was designed for the specific purpose of marinating and dressing sashimi slices. The cubic thicknesss allows the outer layers of the fish to soak up the marinade flavors while the fish maintains its own flavor on the inside of the cube.

Fish with soft, thick flesh, such as tuna, salmon, king fish and bonito are suitable for cubic sashimi. Buy a block approximately 2 x 2 inches (5 x 5 cm) thick and 8 inches (20 cm) in length. A red tuna block of this size would serve 4 people (8 pieces per person). Slice straight down through the flesh and cut block in half lengthwise to make 2 long pieces. Cut each piece in half lengthwise to make 4 long pieces. Then, trim each piece into 1-inch (2.5-cm) cubes, sliding the blade along the flesh.

New-style sashimi

Sashimi chefs make many kinds of decorative sashimi to celebrate special occasions. They use themes and motifs to suit the event, including flowers, fruits and animals; mythological and popular characters; and traditional, seasonal and religious items, all of which are created using sushi rice and other ingredients.

The sashimi chef also uses his artistic skills to make beautiful centerpieces for sashimi platters, all to add to the enjoyment of the dining experience. With a little practice and imagination, you too can soon master and create some of the beautiful ideas in this section as well as your own.

Blanched cuttlefish with aonori

Makes 4 servings

4 cuttlefish
1 tablespoon aonori (flaked green nori)
4 lemon wedges
pine sprigs, for decoration
Japanese soy sauce, for serving

Clean cuttlefish (see page 69), and cut in half vertically. Place 1 piece at a time, outside surface down, and score inside vertically, spacing scoring every $^1/_4$ inch (6 mm). Turn 90 degrees and score again, making a crosshatch pattern. Refrigerate until cooled. Take out and place in the center of a plate, then sprinkle with aonori. Place pine sprigs on one side of the cuttlefish. Garnish with a wedge of lemon.

Serve with soy sauce.

Tip
If aonori is unavailable, chopped chives can be used instead.

Crabmeat with wasabi mayonnaise

Makes 4 servings

1 tablespoon sake
1 tablespoon salt
8 fresh Alaskan (snow) crab sticks
iced water, for chilling
4 strips of daikon 4 inches x ¹/₂ inch (10 cm x 1 cm)
16 long chives, stemmed
¹/₄ punnet mustard cress

Wasabi mayonnaise
1³/₄ oz (50 g) light mayonnaise
¹/₃ oz (10 g) wasabi paste

Bring a pot of water to a boil and add sake and salt. Wrap the sticks of crabmeat with a cotton cloth, and tie so they don't come apart, then boil. When cloth floats to the surface, remove crab and place in iced water. Unwrap the crab legs once they have cooled.

Mix wasabi and mayonnaise to a smooth consistency. Cut each crab stick in half. Tie 2 crab sticks together with 4 pieces chives. Place a tied crab stick to stand on cut end on each bowl, and top with wasabi mayonnaise, daikon strip and mustard cress.

Tip
Lobster meat can be used instead of crabmeat.

Kaki-oyster cocktail

Makes 4 servings

3 cups (24 fl oz/750 ml) water
1 tablespoon salt
8 oysters
2 nori sheets, quartered
4 tablespoons grated chili and daikon
1 tablespoon tobiko (flying fish roe)
8 chive stems, halved
1³/₄ oz (50 g) ugo (salted seaweed)
1³/₄ oz (50 g) shredded daikon

Vinaigrette mixture
2 tablespoons rice vinegar
1 teaspoon sugar
¹/₂ teaspoon mirin
2 drops Japanese soy sauce

Combine all ingredients for vinaigrette mixture in a bowl. Set aside. Place water in bowl and stir in salt.

To shuck oysters: Using an oyster opener or a butter knife, hold oyster in palm of one hand and insert knife into the shell where it is joined together like a hinge. Push against the hinge and twist knife to open shells.

Dip oysters in salted water to enhance texture. Shape each piece of nori into a cylinder and seal using water. Place oyster in cylinder and cylinder in oyster shell. Place grated chili and daikon in shell. Arrange tobiko between daikon and oyster. Insert 2 chive stems in tobiko. Arrange ugo and shredded daikon in the center of each plate. Top with the oyster cocktail in the center of ugo and daikon bed. Drizzle with vinaigrette mixture.

Marinated yellowtail

Makes 4 servings

1 yellow (brown) onion
4 whole yellowtail
1²/₃ oz (50 g) green ginger, grated
1 clove garlic, crushed
1 scallion (shallot/spring onion) stem, finely chopped
4 shiso leaves
2 myoga, halved
3¹/₂ oz (100 g) shredded daikon
4 red radish baskets with wasabi
²/₃ oz (20 g) wasabi paste

Vinaigrette mixture
¹/₂ cup (4 fl oz/125 ml) rice vinegar
2 tablespoons sugar
1 pinch salt
1 teaspoon mirin

Slice onion. Place slices in a bowl of iced water. Fillet yellowtail (see page 40) and cut into small squares, approximately ¹/₂ inch (1 cm) wide. Drain sliced onion.

In a bowl, add all vinegar ingredients and mix until well combined.

Place sliced onion, grated ginger, crushed garlic and chopped scallion in a bowl. Pour in vinegar mixture and mix using chopsticks or a fork. Add yellowtail pieces and mix gently. Remove pieces and place on a board, then lightly grind (mince) with the back of a knife blade to absorb the flavor. Lay a shiso leaf on each plate or bowl with crushed ice, then arrange yellowtail pieces on each plate or bowl and top with condiments from the vinegar mixture. Garnish with a half myoga leaf and 1 radish basket per plate.

Sashimi in lime baskets

Makes 4 servings

4 large limes
4 thin slices snapper
4 okra slices
4 cooked jumbo shrimp (king prawns)
4 salmon strips, 1 inch (2.5 cm) long
4 nori squares 1$^{1}/_{4}$ inch x 1$^{1}/_{4}$ inch (3 cm x 3 cm)
bamboo sprigs
pesticide-free flowers, for decoration

With a small knife or zester, remove narrow strips of peel from lime, working end to end. Cut blossom end of each lime, creating a lid. Scoop out lime with a spoon, leaving a shell. Roll up a snapper piece and place in each basket, then top with an okra slice. Insert a cooked shrimp in basket. Roll salmon strip with nori and trim, then place in basket. Decorate with a bamboo sprig and a flower.

Scallop sashimi

Makes 4 servings

8 scallops
3 cups (24 fl oz/750 ml) salt water
1 tablespoon salt
4 tablespoons salmon caviar

Green tea mixture
1 tablespoon green tea powder
1 tablespoon white miso
1 teaspoon mirin

Rinse scallop shells before using. Insert butter knife in shell and open. Do not discard remaining shells, as they will be used for presentation.

Cut out meat and place in a bowl and add salt. Dip scallops in salted water. In another bowl, combine all ingredients for green tea mixture. Divide tea mixture among 4 half-shells. Place 2 scallops in each shell. Top with caviar.

Tip
Abalone can be used instead of scallops.

Snapper with grapefruit and emerald sauce

Makes 4 servings

7 oz (220 g) snapper fillet, skin removed
1 grapefruit
2 kiwifruits
4 mint leaves, for decoration

Slice snapper fillet into 24 pieces. Starting from the left of the fillet, cut into diagonal slices, inclining the blade to the right at a 45-degree angle. Once the fish is cut, raise the blade to a 90-degree angle and slide each slice to the left.

Cut off ends of grapefruit. Stand on a board and slice off peel and rind. Remove all white pith. Holding grapefruit, cut into 8 sections, removing rind between sections.

Peel kiwifruits and puree in blender. Place about 6 snapper slices on each plate and top with 2 grapefruit pieces. Drip kiwifruit puree around fish with a teaspoon. Top with mint leaf.

Tip
Jewfish and lemon sole can be used instead of snapper.

Whitebait sashimi

Makes 4 servings

$1/4$ cup (2 fl oz/60 ml) rice vinegar
4 kelp sheets, 1 inch x 4 inches (2.5 cm x 10 cm)
10 oz (300 g) whitebait
1 tablespoon mirin
4 carrot strips (with peeler, peel 8 inches/20 cm long)
4 bamboo sprigs, for decoration
wasabi paste, for serving
Japanese soy sauce, for serving

Bring saucepan of salted water to a boil. Place rice vinegar in a
bowl. Dip kelp sheets in boiling water. Remove and place in
rice vinegar. Top with whitebait and sprinkle with mirin. Arrange
a carrot strip and a bamboo sprig.
　Serve with wasabi and soy sauce.

Tip
Small shrimp (prawns) can be used instead of whitebait.

Sauces, condiments and accompaniments

Once, not many people would have considered eating sushi without soy sauce or wasabi, but there is now a wide range of other sauces and accompaniments that works well with sushi. Our world has become smaller and the availability of its many food sources has increased dramatically. These days we find ingredients combined in sushi that had not previously been dreamed of, including cilantro (fresh coriander), Thai basil, chili, fish sauce, and coconut, which all have flavors that are very compatible with sushi.

Combining sushi with condiments or sauces adds flavor. Even strong-flavored fish, such as bonito, yellowtail and garfish, also benefit from this addition. You can create an enormous range of dressed dishes using the many varieties of fish, the different slicing techniques, and the numerous condiments and sauces. There is a wide variety of pickled vegetables and fresh or seasoned ingredients and condiments that will expand the variety of sushi and complement its delicate flavors.

Black sesame paste (Goma-dare)

Makes 4 servings

¹/₄ **cup black sesame seeds, toasted**
2 tablespoons mirin
1 teaspoon green-ginger juice (see page 235)

Grind sesame seeds, using a mortar and pestle, gradually adding mirin and green-ginger juice. Mix until smooth. Use as an accompaniment to steamed sashimi.

Chili soy sauce

Japanese soy sauce
shichimi togarashi (7 spice mix) or fresh red chili, seeded and finely sliced

Combine soy sauce with schichimi togarashi or fresh chili, to taste.

Cucumber pickles (Kyuri no shiomomi)

Makes 4 servings

10 oz (300 g) English (hothouse) cucumber, thinly sliced
3¹/₂ oz (105 g) cabbage, finely shredded
¹/₂-inch (1 cm) piece peeled fresh ginger, cut into fine
  matchstick strips
1¹/₂ teaspoons salt
sesame seeds, for garnish

In a bowl, gently mix all ingredients except sesame seeds.
Cover with plastic wrap, pressing it down on surface of
ingredients. Fill a smaller bowl with water and place on covered
ingredients to apply weight. Let stand for 1 hour. Remove bowl
of water. Drain liquid from cucumber pickles, garnish with
sesame seeds and serve.

Daikon pickles with bonito (Daikon no tosazuke)

Makes 4 servings

1 lb (500 g) daikon
2 teaspoons salt
3 daikon leaves, blanched then finely sliced
1¹/₄-inch (3-cm) piece peeled fresh ginger, finely grated
¹/₆ oz (5 g) bonito flakes
black sesame seeds, for garnish
Japanese soy sauce, for serving

Peel daikon and cut lengthwise into quarters. Thinly slice each
quarter. Place daikon in a bowl and mix in salt. Set aside until
daikon softens, 10–15 minutes. Gently squeeze daikon with your
hands, drain liquid, then add sliced leaves. Cover with plastic
wrap, pressing it down on surface of ingredients. Fill a smaller
bowl with water and place on ingredients to apply weight. Let
stand for 1 hour. Remove bowl of water. Squeeze as much liquid
as possible from daikon. Place daikon pickles in 4 bowls. Top
with ginger and bonito flakes and sprinkle with sesame seeds.

Egg-yolk vinaigrette (Kimizu)

Makes 4 servings

4 egg yolks, beaten
1 tablespoon rice vinegar
1 teaspoon mirin

In a bowl, whisk egg yolk and rice vinegar. Add mirin and whisk together. Sieve mixture well. Egg-yolk vinaigrette is used as a dressing or as a dipping sauce for sashimi slices made with white-fleshed fish, such as snapper, silver bream and John Dory.

Ginger sesame sauce

Makes 1 cup (8 fl oz/250 ml)

1–2 teaspoons ginger juice, to taste
1/2 cup (4 fl oz/125 ml) Japanese soy sauce
1/4 cup (2 fl oz/60 ml) mirin
1/4 cup (2 fl oz/60 ml) sake
1/2 teaspoon Asian sesame oil

To obtain ginger juice: Finely grate fresh ginger and squeeze to extract ginger juice. Alternatively, use grated fresh ginger in recipe, but decrease to about 1/2 teaspoon or to taste.

In a small bowl, combine ginger juice, soy sauce, mirin, sake, and sesame oil. Stir well. Refrigerate until needed.

Grated chili and daikon (Momiji-oroshi)

Makes 4 servings

7 oz (220 g) daikon
2 small red chili peppers

Peel daikon and trim ends. Make 2 small holes in ends with chopsticks, large enough for a chili pepper. Insert 1 chili into each hole. Grate daikon and mix gently in a bowl.

The combination of hot chili and bitter daikon refreshes the palate and is especially suited to light-tasting sashimi, such as usu-zukuri (paper-thin sashimi) with a vinaigrette sauce. It is particularly good for white-fleshed fish.

Miso sesame sauce

Makes $3/4$ cup (6 fl oz/180 ml)

$1/4$ cup (2 fl oz/60 ml) rice vinegar
2 tablespoons water or number-one dashi stock
  (see page 152)
1 tablespoon white miso paste
1 tablespoon sesame seed paste
  or tahini
1 tablespoon sugar
1 teaspoon toasted white
  sesame seeds
1 scallion (shallot/spring onion), green part only, thinly sliced

In a small bowl, combine rice vinegar, water, miso, sesame seed paste and sugar, stirring well until sugar dissolves. Cover and refrigerate until required. Garnish with sesame seeds and scallion.

This sesame sauce can be made 2–3 days ahead and refrigerated until needed. Add finely chopped chili or wasabi for extra bite.

Green tea miso (Maccha miso)

Makes 4 servings

1 tablespoon maccha (green
  tea powder)
$1^1/2$ teaspoons white miso
2 teaspoons mirin

In a bowl, mix tea powder, miso and mirin, and whisk together until well combined.

Marinade for vegetables

1 tablespoon rice vinegar
2 tablespoon vegetable oil
1 teaspoon sesame oil
1 teaspoon Japanese soy sauce
pinch salt

This marinade is ideal for blanched green beans, snow peas (mange-tout), spinach, carrots, sweet peppers and tofu. Use the vegetables in sushi rolls or chirashi-zushi.

In a small bowl, combine vinegar, oils, soy sauce and salt.

Pickled carrot and daikon

1 medium carrot
3-inch (7.5-cm) piece daikon
1 teaspoon salt
3 tablespoons rice vinegar
1/2 teaspoon Japanese soy sauce
1/8 teaspoon peeled and grated fresh ginger
2 teaspoons sugar

Peel and finely shred carrot and daikon. Put into large bowl, sprinkle with salt and let stand for 30 minutes. Gently squeeze out as much water as possible from vegetables. In a bowl, combine vinegar, soy sauce, ginger and sugar, stirring until sugar dissolves. Add vegetables and refrigerate for 8 hours. Pickled carrot and daikon will keep for 1 week if refrigerated in an airtight container.

Quick variation: Soak shredded carrot and daikon separately for 15 minutes in cold water. Drain well and sprinkle with sushi vinegar before serving.

Pickled cucumber

1 English (hothouse) cucumber, thinly sliced
2 teaspoons salt
1/4 cup (2 fl oz/60 ml) sushi vinegar (see brown sushi rice page 44)

Put cucumbers in a bowl, sprinkle with salt and let stand for 5 minutes. Rinse under cold water to remove salt. Sprinkle with sushi vinegar and refrigerate overnight. Serve in a small bowl. If a milder vinegar flavor is preferred, heat the vinegar for 1 minute.

Pickled ginger

3–4 pieces fresh ginger, peeled and thinly sliced along the grain
salt
1/2 cup (4 fl oz/125 ml) rice vinegar
2 tablespoons sugar, or to taste
1/4 cup (2 fl oz/60 ml) water

Pickled ginger will keep for several months if refrigerated in an airtight container. Allow 1–2 tablespoons per person for a sushi meal. Eat with fingers or chopsticks.

Spread ginger slices in a colander and sprinkle with salt. Let stand until soft, 30 minutes or longer. Drop ginger into boiling water to blanch. Drain and cool. In a bowl, combine rice vinegar, sugar and water, stirring well until sugar dissolves. Add ginger and refrigerate until well seasoned, about 1 day. The ginger will turn pinkish in the marinade. For more color, add a drop of pink food coloring to the marinade.

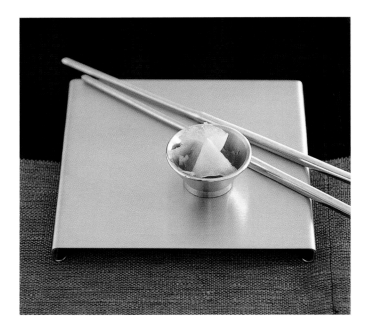

Sauces and pastes

Aonori (seaweed) paste
Made from seaweed, this is particularly good with cooked rice. Sold in bottles in Japanese markets.

Chili mayonnaise (see picture at top)
This is chili added to Japanese mayonnaise. Use either chili paste or fresh chilies, and add as much or as little as desired. Chili mayonnaise is particularly suitable for chicken.

Fish sauce
Pungent sauce of salted, fermented fish and other seasonings, used in cooking and as a dipping sauce. Products vary in intensity, based on the country of origin.

Green curry paste
This is suitable for sushi made with fresh vegetables or fruit.

Honey chili sauce
Available bottled from Asian or Japanese markets. Refrigerate after opening.

Japanese mayonnaise (see picture at center)
Japanese mayonnaise is suitable for a large variety of ingredients. It is less tangy than western mayonnaise. For more bite add wasabi to make wasabi mayonnaise.

Mango chutney (see picture over page at top)
This is a popular accompaniment to Indian curries. It has a sweet and sour taste and complements rice particularly well. Add to sushi in small amounts.

Nihaizu
This soy and vinegar dipping sauce is made by combining 1/2 cup (4 fl oz/125 ml) tosa shoyu (see page 228) with 1/2 cup (4 fl oz/125 ml) rice vinegar and 1 teaspoon mirin and mixing well. It will keep for up to 2 months in the refrigerator.

Pistachio and peanut sate sauce (see picture at bottom)
This spicy, peanut-flavored sauce is a favorite in Indonesia. It is a mixture of peanut butter and crushed peanuts, sprinkled with chopped pistachio.

Ponzu sauce
Combine 1/2 cup (4 fl oz/125 ml) each of daidai or lemon juice, Japanese soy sauce and number-one dashi (see page 152) and mix well. This sauce keep for up to 2 months in the refrigerator.

Soy sauce (shoyu)
Soy sauce is essential to Japanese cuisine. Made from soybeans and salt, it is used in cooking and as a dipping sauce for sushi and other dishes.

Sumiso sauce

In a saucepan over a high heat, combine 1/2 cup (2 fl oz/60 ml) shiromiso (see page 236), 2 tablespoons each of sugar, sake and water, 1 1/2 tablespoons rice vinegar and 2 teaspoons hot English mustard. Bring to a boil, stirring frequently. Remove from heat and let cool before serving. Keeps well for up to 2 months in the refrigerator.

Sweet and sour chili sauce

Available in bottles, from Asian markets, this is a very popular sauce in Asian countries. It is particularly suitable for pork dishes.

Tempura sauce

In a saucepan over high heat, combine 1 cup (8 fl oz/250 ml) number-one dashi (see page 152) and 1/4 cup (2 fl oz/60 ml) each of Japanese soy sauce and mirin. Bring to a boil then remove from heat. Allow to cool before serving. This sauce keeps well for up to 3 days in the refrigerator.

Teriyaki sauce

In a saucepan over a high heat, combine 1 cup (8 fl oz/250ml) each of Japanese soy sauce and brown sugar with 2 tablespoons chicken stock and 1 teaspoon mirin. Bring to a boil and simmer for 5 minutes, being careful not to let sauce boil over. Serve hot. Keeps well for up to 2 months in the refrigerator.

Tosa shoyu

This mildly sweet soy variation is also used quite often with sashimi. Put 3 tablespoons Japanese soy sauce, 3 tablespoon bonito flakes, 1 tablespoon sake and 1/2 teaspoon mirin (optional) in a small saucepan and bring to the boil, stirring constantly. Strain through a fine sieve over a bowl. Allow to cool.

Wasabi

Wasabi is a native Japanese plant found growing near clear spring water. The root is grated and used as a condiment for sushi, sashimi, or soba noodles. Because of its distinctive pungent taste, it is often called Japanese mustard or horseradish. Wasabi is eaten with raw fish because it is believed to kill germs and parasites. It is available in both paste and powder forms.

As well as being used inside sushi rolls, wasabi can be served on the side. Its attractive green color lends itself to many decorative effects. Some people like to dip their sushi directly into the wasabi, but usually a small amount is picked up with chopsticks and mixed into a dish of soy sauce to use as a tangy dipping sauce.

Similar products with a "bite," such as chili or red horseradish sauce, may be used as a substitute for wasabi. It is best used sparingly, as the tang should add a subtle dimension to food and never dominate it.

Seasoned carrots

1 medium carrot, peeled and cut into thin strips
1/3 cup (3 fl oz/90 ml) dashi stock (see page 152) or water
2 teaspoons sugar
1 teaspoon light Japanese soy sauce
pinch salt

In a small saucepan combine dashi, sugar, soy sauce and salt. Simmer over low heat until carrot is tender and most of the liquid is absorbed. Remove using a slotted spoon and set aside to cool.

Seasoned lotus root

2 oz (60 g) lotus root, peeled and cut into 1/8-inch (5-mm) slices
2 tablespoons sugar
3 tablespoons rice vinegar
1/2 teaspoon salt

Soak lotus root water and rice vinegar to prevent discoloration. In a saucepan, bring remaining ingredients to a boil. Add the lotus slices and simmer for 8–10 minutes. Drain.

Seasoned kampyo

Makes 18

1 oz (30 g) kampyo
1 cup (8 fl oz/250 ml) dashi stock (see page 152) or water
2 tablespoons sugar
2 teaspoons sake
2 tablespoons Japanese soy sauce

Wash kampyo in cold water and salt, gently rubbing the strips together. Drain and wash again. Alternatively, soak in water to soften for 2 hours or longer. Place kampyo and water in a saucepan and gently boil until tender, about 10 minutes. Drain well. In a saucepan, bring

kampyo, dashi, sugar, sake and soy sauce to a boil. Reduce heat and simmer for 15 minutes. Remove from heat and cool in liquid. Drain and cut into 8-inch (20-cm) lengths.

Seasoned shiitake mushrooms

6 dried shiitake mushrooms
1/2 cup (4 fl oz/125 ml) dashi stock (see page 101) or water
1 1/2 tablespoons caster sugar
1 1/2 tablespoons Japanese soy sauce
2 tablespoons mirin

Cover mushrooms in warm water until softened, 20–30 minutes. Remove using a slotted spoon. Use seasoned liquid in soups and other dishes. Discard stems and slice thinly or keep mushroom caps whole, depending on use. Place in a saucepan with remaining ingredients and

simmer for 10 minutes. Remove using a slotted spoon. Use seasoned liquid to flavor cooked rice.

Teas

Chrysanthemum flower tea

In Japan, fresh chrysanthemum flowers are used in sashimi, tempura, and soup. Chrysanthemum tea can also be made by pouring hot water on a couple of dried flowers. Combining it with a small amount of green or black tea helps to moderate the strong flavor. The flowers are available from Japanese or other Asian markets.

Green tea

In sushi bar terms, green tea is called agari, which means "a finish." In between sushi varieties, green tea is drunk to cleanse the palette to aid diners to appreciate the flavor of the next sushi roll. Green tea is the national beverage of Japan. Once the leaves of the tea bushes are picked, they are immediately steamed. This prevents the leaves from turning black, so the result is green tea. The syllable cha on the end of a word (or ocha, when it stands alone) means "tea."

There are a number of varieties of green teas, such as gyokuro, sencha, bancha, matcha (powdered green tea), genmaicha, and hojicha. The most economical tea is bancha; bancha means "late harvest" and is made from large, hard leaves, including the stems and red stalks. Because the flavor is weaker, it is suitable for children. Sencha is available in a wide variety of qualities and prices. Average-quality sencha of the large leaf variety is intended for everyday use and is commonly found in homes and offices. Gyokuro is the very best of Japan's teas. It has a delicate flavor that epitomizes the uniqueness of Japanese flavor. Depending on quality, the water temperature and length of infusion should be adjusted accordingly. Genmaicha is bancha made with hulled rice kernels, which adds an interesting flavor. These are both medium-quality teas that yield a light brown, refreshing infusion with a slightly savory flavor. It is rich in vitamins.

Hojicha

Hojicha was invented in 1920 by a merchant in Kyoto who did not know what to do with a surplus stock of leaves. He had the idea of roasting them and so created a tea with a new flavor. The lightly roasted leaves yield a light brown tea with a distinctive flavor.

Thick seasoned omelette (Tamago-yaki)

Makes 2 omelettes

8 large eggs, lightly beaten
2 tablespoons dashi stock or water (see page 152)
2 tablespoons sugar
1 tablespoon mirin
1 tablespoon light Japanese soy sauce
1/4 teaspoon salt
1–2 tablespoons vegetable oil
1/2 cup grated daikon, drained
Japanese soy sauce

Combine eggs, dashi, sugar, mirin, soy sauce and salt in a bowl, stirring well until sugar dissolves, and divide mixture in half. Heat an 8-inch (20-cm) square omelette pan, small frying pan or skillet over moderate-low heat. Coat with a thin layer of oil, wiping excess with paper towel. Cover frying pan thinly with egg mixture, tilting pan to spread evenly to each corner. Break any air bubbles with chopsticks so omelette lies flat. When almost set, run chopsticks around the edges to loosen egg from pan, then lift egg on the side furthest away from you and fold into thirds towards the front of the pan. Gently push folded omelette to back of pan. Lightly grease pan with paper towel and repeat the procedure, lifting up cooked egg so mixture runs underneath. When nearly cooked, fold in thirds starting with the egg already folded. Repeat for remaining mixture lightly greasing pan between batches.

While hot, tip omelette onto a bamboo mat and wrap firmly, forming a compact rectangular shape. Cool and cut as required. Repeat with remaining half mixture. Serve with daikon and soy sauce.

Thin seasoned omelette (Usuyaki tamago)

Makes about 8 omelettes

6 eggs
1 tablespoon mirin
1 tablespoon sugar
1/4 teaspoon salt
1–2 teaspoons vegetable oil

Gently beat eggs with mirin, sugar and salt, without creating big air bubbles. Strain mixture to remove any strands of egg. Lightly grease an 8-inch (20-cm) square or 9-inch (23-cm) round frying pan or skillet with oil, wiping any excess with paper towel. Heat oiled pan on moderate-low until a drop of water flicked onto surface skips across surface and evaporates quickly.

Cover frying pan thinly with egg mixture, tilting pan to spread evenly into each corner. Break any air bubbles with chopsticks so omelette lies flat. When almost set and surface begins to look firm and slightly dry, run chopsticks around edges to loosen egg from pan. Flip omelette over and cook other side for only a few seconds, being careful not to overcook. Remove to a plate. Repeat for remaining mixture, lightly greasing pan between each batch. If a round frying pan is used, omelettes may be trimmed to a square shape as required.

Tips
- To use for nigiri-zushi, cut omelette across into 1/2-inch (1 cm) slices or cut lengthwise into long thin strips, 1/2 inch (1 cm) wide, to use as a filling for sushi rolls.
- To use as a side dish to accompany sushi, serve seasoned omelette with soy sauce and grated daikon .

Suggested serving sizes

Sushi type	Fillings	Nori	Sushi rice (cooked)
Large sushi roll (Futomaki-zushi)	5–6	1 sheet	1 cup
Small sushi roll (Hosomaki-zushi)	1–2	½ sheet	1/2 cup
Inside-out sushi roll (Uramaki-zushi)	3–4	½ sheet	¾ cup
Topping on rice ball (Nigiri-zushi)	1 slice or topping		1½ tablespoons (6–7 per cup)
Seasoned tofu pouches (Inari-zushi)			2 tablespoons (5 per cup)
Hand-wrapped sushi (Temaki-zushi)	2–4	¼ or ½	1½ tablespoons (6–7 per cup)
Battleship sushi (Gunkan maki-zushi)	1 topping	1 strip, 1 inch by 5 inches (2 cm by 13 cm)	1½ tablespoons (2 teaspoons for mini size)

Mixed plate

4 Nigiri-zushi

1 small roll (hosomaki-zushi) (6 pieces)

2 battleship sushi (gunkan maki-zushi)

1 seasoned tofu pouch (inari-zushi)

OR

1 small roll (hosomaki-zushi) (6 pieces)

½ large sushi roll (futomaki-zushi) (4 pieces)

2 seasoned tofu pouches (inari-zushi)

Type of Sushi		Sushi for 2	Sushi for 4	Sushi for 6–8
(1 cup prepared sushi rice = 150 g)				
Large sushi roll	No. rolls (8 pieces)	2 (16 pieces)	4 (32 pieces)	6–8 (48–64 pieces)
(Futomaki-zushi)	Sushi rice (cups)	2	4	6–8
	Nori sheets	2	4	6–8
	Fillings	2 x 5–6	4 x 5–6	6–8 x 5–6
Small sushi roll	No. rolls (6 pieces)	4 (24 pieces)	8 (48 pieces)	12–16 (72–96 pieces)
(Hosomaki-zushi)	Sushi rice (cups)	2	4	6–8
	Nori sheets	2	4	6–8
	No. fillings	4 x 1–2	8 x 1–2	12–16 x 1–2
Inside-out sushi roll	No. rolls (8 pieces)	3	6	9–12
(Uramaki-zushi)	Sushi rice (cups)	2$\frac{1}{4}$	4$\frac{1}{2}$	7–9
	Nori sheets	1$\frac{1}{2}$	3	4$\frac{1}{2}$–6
	No. fillings	3 x 4–5	6 x 4–5	9–12 x 4–5
Nigiri-zushi	No.	20	40	60–80
(topping on rice ball)	Sushi rice	3 cups	6 cups	9–12 cups
	Toppings	20	40	60–80
Seasoned tofu pouches	No. pouches	6	12	18–24
(Inari-zushi)	Sushi rice	12 tablespoons	24 tablespoons	36–48 tablespoons
	2 tablespoons per pouch (5 per cup)	(1$\frac{1}{4}$ cups)	(2$\frac{1}{2}$ cups)	(4–5 cups)
	Ties			
	(seasoned kampyo)	6	12	18–24
Hand-wrapped sushi	No.	18	36	54–72
(Temaki-zushi)	Sushi rice	3 cups	5$\frac{1}{2}$ cups	8–11 cups
	No. fillings	18 x 2–4	36 x 2–4	45–72 x 2–4
Battleship sushi	No.	6	12	18–24
(Gunkan maki-zushi)	Sushi rice	1 cup	2 cups	3–3$\frac{3}{4}$ cups

Glossary

Abura-age: Thinly sliced, deep-fried tofu. Pour boiling water over tofu or simmer in boiling water for 1–2 minutes and gently squeeze to remove excess oil and water before use. See Seasoned tofu.

Aka oroshi: Japanese red chili paste. This is mixed with grated daikon radish and used as a garnish for white-fish sushi. Do not substitute other types of chili paste, as they will probably be too pungent. Alternatively, push a few dried red chilies into a piece of daikon and grate finely or sprinkle chili flakes over grated daikon.

Ao-nori: Edible green seaweed. Sold in dried flake form. It is usually sprinkled when served, so it is not too moist when eaten.

Asian sesame oil: A fragrant, richly colored oil made from sesame seeds. Has a darker, stronger flavor and fragrance than the lighter one. Only small quantities of Asian sesame oil are required for flavoring.

Bamboo leaves: Inedible garnish, often used when fish is placed on top of leaf. Bamboo leaves need sustained moisture and should be kept in water until needed.

Bamboo shoots: Tender but crispy shoots, available in cans from most stores. Used for texture rather than flavor.

Beni-shoga: Pickled red ginger made with older season ginger. More savory than the pink variety (gari). Available sliced or shredded in packets or jars.

Blanched cabbage leaves: Rinse leaves to remove dirt and microwave 1–2 minutes, or simmer in boiling water until leaves just softened, 1–2 minutes. Immediately rinse under cold water to stop the cooking process.

Blanched spinach leaves: Rinse leaves to remove dirt and mircowave 1–2 minutes, or simmer in boiling water until leaves just softened, 1–2 minutes. Immediately rinse under cold water to stop the cooking process and set color.

Bonito flakes: These large sandy brown flakes of smoked and dried bonito fish are used to make dashi, which is a basic Japanese stock. The small flakes, sold in small cellophane packets, are used as a garnish.

Cellophane noodles: Also known as bean thread or harusame noodles. Gossamer, translucent threads are made from the starch of green mung beans, potato starch or sweet potato starch. They are sold dried and so must be soaked in hot water to soften before using.

Chili mayonnaise: This is chili added to Japanese mayonnaise. Use either chili paste or fresh chilies, and add as much or as little as desired. Chili mayonnaise is particularly suitable for chicken.

Chili oil: Vegetable oil infused with chilies to obtain their flavor and heat. Often tinged red, there are many varieties of chili oil available in both Asian markets and supermarkets. It will keep for up to 6 months at room temperature, but retains its flavor better if stored in the refrigerator.

Chili peppers: As a general rule, the smaller the chili the hotter the flavor regardless of the color. Remove seeds and membranes to reduce heat.

Chili sauce or sweet chili sauce: Although not traditional, this spicy blend of tomatoes, chilies and onions can be used as a dipping sauce in or with sushi.

Chinese napa cabbage: Although closely related to bok choy or pak choi, Chinese cabbage or wong bok looks more like an elongated Western cabbage. It has a crisp texture, high water content, and a delicate, almost sweet flavor.

Cilantro: Also known as coriander or Chinese parsley. Available fresh, the roots, stems and leaves are all used in cooking. The leaves are used for garnishing and are strongly flavored, so use sparingly.

Dashi: This traditional Japanese stock, which is made from bonito fish flakes (katsuobushi) and konbu (seaweed), is the basis of many Japanese dishes. Granules or liquid instant dashi is readily available. If a completely vegetarian stock is required, use only konbu and double the quantity.

Dried somen noodles: Thin, white noodles made from wheat flour.

Egg mimosa: Sieved egg yolk cooked until hard (hard-boiled), used for sprinkling or a decoration such as the stamen in a carved radish flower. To make a teaspoon of egg mimosa, place a fresh egg in a pot of water. Bring water to a boil and simmer for 15 minutes until egg is hard-boiled. Remove egg shell under running water and when egg is chilled, remove egg white. Place egg yolk in a sieve. Pressing with a teaspoon, sieve into a small bowl.

Enoki mushrooms: Also called enokitake mushrooms, these are pale colored with long thin stalks topped by tiny caps. They have a mild flavor and crunchy texture. Fresh mushrooms may be purchased in Asian markets and some supermarkets. Trim the root ends of the stalks before using.

Fish sauce: Pungent sauce of salted, fermented fish and other seasonings, used in cooking and as a dipping sauce. Products vary in intensity based on the country of origin.

Fu: Wheat gluten in small decorative shapes. Sold dried.

Gari: Pickled pink ginger made with early season ginger. Sweeter than the red variety (beni-shoga). Available sliced in packets and jars. Served with sushi for cleansing the palate in between dishes.

Green curry paste: This is suitable for sushi made with fresh vegetables or fruit.

Green-ginger juice: Peel a green ginger and grate into a bowl. Squeeze with fingers to make green-ginger juice.

Ichimi togarashi: Ground chili powder used as a seasoning (see also shichimi togarashi).

Japanese mayonnaise: Japanese mayonnaise is creamy and less sweet than western mayonnaise. For more bite add wasabi to make wasabi mayonnaise.

Kanten (agar): Also called agar-agar, this is a tasteless dried seaweed used as a setting agent, much like gelatine. It is available in blocks, powders or strands, from Asian supermarkets, healthfood stores and some large supermarkets.

Kelp: Large dark brown seaweed sold dry. When using, rinse kelp and soak in water. Kelp is highly nutritious, but it is seldom eaten on its own.

Kinome: Japanese pepper; the sprigs provide an aromatic additional flavor. They are an edible garnish or herbal ingredient.

Konbu: Also known as kombu. This dried giant kelp or seaweed is available in the form of hard, flat black sheets that often have a fine white powder on the surface. Avoid konbu that is wrinkled and thin. Konbu is used to flavor dashi, a basic soup stock, and sushi rice. Washing before use results in lost flavor, so wipe the surface of the sheets with a damp cloth instead. Cut edges or cut into pieces to release extra flavor. Should be removed from stock before boiling or taste becomes bitter.

Konnyaku: Devil's tongue jelly. Made from konnyaku potato and formed either into bricks or strings.

Maccha: Green tea, a green powdered tea with a bitter yet pleasant taste. This tea is indispensable in a Japanese tea ceremony.

Miso: Made by fermenting soybean paste and wheat barley or rice. Full of protein. Many varieties are available, including red, white, salt-reduced, and some mixed with other cereals (e.g. rice). The general rule is the darker the color, the saltier the taste. Light and dark can be mixed for interesting flavors. White miso (see **shiromiso**) has a lighter taste and less salt. Usually used in dressings or as sauce for sashimi. Better to use with blue cheese puree because of its contrasting color.

Mitsuba: Used as a herb in soups and salads, mitsuba, also known as Japanese wild chervil, is a form of parsley, which can be substituted. The tastes, however, are not identical; the flavor of mitsuba is somewhat like that of celery.

Myoga: Japanese ginger, but has quite a different herbal fragrance than ginger when sliced thinly as a sashimi condiment.

Rice vinegar: Vinegar fermented from rice, and fairly mild in flavor. Rice vinegar matches sushi rice and other dishes perfectly.

Sansho: Japanese pepper, bitter tasting.

Seasoned tofu (seasoned abura-age): Thinly sliced, deep-fried tofu that has been simmered in sweetened soy sauce. One side is cut so tofu can be opened to form a pouch which can be stuffed with sushi rice.

Shichimi togarashi: Seven spice mix, based on hot peppers. Used as a seasoning.

Shimeji mushrooms: Clusters of straw-colored mushrooms with small heads. Use in soups and nabemono (one pot dishes).

Shiromiso: White miso, with a pale yellow color, a sweet flavor, and a salt content that varies from 5 to 10 percent.

Shiso: An aromatic herb that belongs to the same family as mint and basil, it is also known as perilla or Japanese basil. Buy fresh green leaves from Asian supermarkets.

Shiitake mushrooms: Available fresh or dried. Dried mushrooms have a more concentrated flavor so use sparingly. Soften dried shiitake in lukewarm water for 30 minutes. Discard stems, as they do not soften.

Soba noodles: Noodles made from buckwheat flour, wheat flour and sometimes powdered green tea.

Sushi vinegar: Mixture of rice vinegar, sugar and salt. Available prepared in liquid or powder form. There are different styles and flavors of sushi vinegar in Japan—some sweet, some salty. The proportions of the three ingredients, rice vinegar, sugar and salt, can be varied according to personal taste. Commercial sushi vinegar can be purchased at most Asian grocery stores and even some larger western supermarkets. Sushi vinegar can be made ahead and refrigerated in an airtight container. If making your own, make sure sugar and salt have dissolved before use.

Takuan: Pickled daikon radish that is colored yellow. Some are flavored with seaweed or chili. Sold whole or sliced in vacuum sealed packs. Keeps well refrigerated after opening. Use in sushi rolls or as a side dish of pickles.

Tempura Flour (tenpura ko): This flour comes in many variations, but is basically a mixture of eggs, wheat flour and iced water. The ingredients are combined only lightly until a lumpy batter full of air bubbles forms. If the batter settles during food preparation, it should be replaced with a new batch.

Tobiko: Preserved flying fish roe. A very thin texture, and a sparkling orange color.

Ugo: salted green seaweed, sold in a packet. Rinse well, before using.

Wakame: A type of seaweed available in dried form that is reconstituted in water and becomes bright green. Wakame is used in soups, salads, simmered dishes, and is finely chopped through rice. Dried wakame must be soaked before using.

Index

Guide to weights & measures

The conversions given in the recipes in this book are approximate. Whichever system you use, remember to follow it consistently, thereby ensuring that the proportions are consistent throughout a recipe.

Weights

Imperial	Metric
$1/3$ oz	10 g
$1/2$ oz	15 g
$3/4$ oz	20 g
1 oz	30 g
2 oz	60 g
3 oz	90 g
4 oz ($1/4$ lb)	125 g
5 oz ($1/3$ lb)	150 g
6 oz	180 g
7 oz	220 g
8 oz ($1/2$ lb)	250 g
9 oz	280 g
10 oz	300 g
11 oz	330 g
12 oz ($3/4$ lb)	375 g
16 oz (1 lb)	500 g
2 lb	1 kg
3 lb	1.5 kg
4 lb	2 kg

Volume

Imperial	Metric	Cup
1 fl oz	30 ml	
2 fl oz	60 ml	$1/4$
3 fl oz	90 ml	$1/3$
4 fl oz	125 ml	$1/2$
5 fl oz	150 ml	$2/3$
6 fl oz	180 ml	$3/4$
8 fl oz	250 ml	1
10 fl oz	300 ml	$1\frac{1}{4}$
12 fl oz	375 ml	$1\frac{1}{2}$
13 fl oz	400 ml	$1\frac{2}{3}$
14 fl oz	440 ml	$1\frac{3}{4}$
16 fl oz	500 ml	2
24 fl oz	750 ml	3
32 fl oz	1L	4

Oven temperature guide

The Celsius (°C) and Fahrenheit (°F) temperatures in this chart apply to most electric ovens. Decrease by 25°F or 10°C for a gas oven or refer to the manufacturer's temperature guide. For temperatures below 325°F (160°C), do not decrease the given temperature.

Oven description	°C	°F	Gas Mark
Cool	110	225	$1/4$
	130	250	$1/2$
Very slow	140	275	1
	150	300	2
Slow	170	325	3
Moderate	180	350	4
	190	375	5
Moderately Hot	200	400	6
Fairly Hot	220	425	7
Hot	230	450	8
Very Hot	240	475	9
Extremely Hot	250	500	10

Useful conversions

$1/4$ teaspoon	1.25 ml
$1/2$ teaspoon	2.5 ml
1 teaspoon	5 ml
1 Australian tablespoon	20 ml (4 teaspoons)
1 UK/US tablespoon	15 ml (3 teaspoons)

Butter/Shortening

1 tablespoon	$1/2$ oz	15 g
$1\frac{1}{2}$ tablespoons	$3/4$ oz	20 g
2 tablespoons	1 oz	30 g
3 tablespoons	$1\frac{1}{2}$ oz	45 g

A LANSDOWNE BOOK

First published in the UK in 2005 by
Apple Press
7 Greendland Street
London NW1 OND
United Kingdom

Reprinted in 2006, 2008, 2010, 2011

www.apple-press.com

Created and produced by Lansdowne Publishing Pty Ltd
Text: Hideo Dekura, Brigid Treloar, Ryuichi Yoshii
Design: Grant Slaney, The Mordern Art ProductionGroup
Photography: Louise Lister, Mark O'Meara
Editor: Joanne Holliman
Production Manager: Sally Stokes
Project Co-ordinator: Kate Merrifield

ISBN: 978-1-84543-066-5

Set in Helvetica on QuarkXPress
Printed in Singapore